TALES FROM THE
SCOTTISH
COUNTRYSIDE

By the same author

Man With Two Dogs – A Breath of Fresh Air from Scotland

Sea Dog Bamse – World War II Canine Hero
(co-authored with Andrew Orr)

TALES FROM THE SCOTTISH COUNTRYSIDE

New Walks with the Man with Two Dogs

ANGUS WHITSON

BLACK & WHITE PUBLISHING

First published 2009
by Black & White Publishing Ltd
29 Ocean Drive, Edinburgh EH6 6JL

1 3 5 7 9 10 8 6 4 2   09 10 11 12 13

ISBN: 978 1 84502 257 0

Typeset by RefineCatch Ltd, Bungay, Suffolk
Printed and bound by MPG Books Ltd

Contents

Acknowledgements

My thanks to:

Dundee *Courier & Advertiser*
for their continued confidence in me
and the opportunity to indulge myself
writing about the countryside

Alan Beattie Herriot,
sculptor, artist and illustrator,
for his humorous cartoonery

niallbenvie.com
for the cover photograph

My love and gratitude
to my wife Liz
for remaining unruffled

Visit the 'Man with two dogs' website to see
every Saturday article published in *The Courier*.
Updated each week.
www.manwithtwodogs.com

To sit with a dog on a hillside on a glorious afternoon
is to be back in Eden, when doing nothing
was not boring – it was peace.

Milan Kundera

Introduction

This is the second collection of articles taken from my weekly countryside diary, now in its seventh year, entitled 'Man with Two Dogs' and published each Saturday in the *Dundee Courier and Advertiser*. Topped up again with reminiscences and comments, feedback from readers and more delicious recipes *From the Doyenne's Kitchen*. The Doyenne, of course, is that 'most respected and prominent woman' in my life – my wife Liz.

The excitement I felt the first Saturday the first article appeared in the newspaper is matched by the pleasure I get each week from the discipline of producing my weekly column. Following the successful format of my first book, *Man with two dogs – A breath of fresh air from Scotland*, this one tracks the seasons of the year and recounts what I and my dogs see and hear, month by month. The dogs accompany me and the Doyenne much of the time and wherever we go in Scotland, and elsewhere, there is always something fresh and interesting to write about.

I welcome each season's progress – each has its own appeal and interest and excites my enthusiasm. Lazy days in summer are fun, but I get bored with too much heat. Gathering autumn's harvest from the garden and the wild is much more satisfying, and we look forward to those days. I never complain about having to wrap up well and go out with the dogs on sharp, crackling winter mornings when the geese are crying overhead in a thin, blue January sky.

But it's the sparkle of green on the emerging leaves, the blues and yellows of the wild flowers, and the lengthening mornings which make it so pleasurable to rise early and, dogs at heel, step out to join the dawn chorus with the sense that there's much more still to come, that makes spring my special season.

In the course of writing my *Courier* column I have said farewell to two dogs. We lost Sheba, our black Labrador, in May 2004 aged fourteen years. She was replaced by Inka, another black Labrador, who sadly died in October 2008. Little Macbeth, our West Highland white terrier, or Westie, seems to be made of old boots because he has survived these crises and is still going strong.

Any apparent confusion about which dogs I have owned from time to time can be explained by remembering that I started off with Sheba and Macbeth. Sheba died. After a break of some months it was Macbeth and Inka, and Inka died. However we are back to full strength now with the arrival in April 2009 of Inka Two. We could hardly call him anything else as he is the first Inka's grandson and is so like his grandfather it's uncanny.

In December 2007 I wrote:

It's almost five years since I began writing these Saturday pieces and I've had some wonderful encounters with nature. Knowing I've had a weekly column to fill and a deadline to meet has made me more conscious of what goes on around me when the dogs and I set out each afternoon. I'm always on the lookout for things to write about; sometimes I've been in the right place at the right time and sometimes it's been sheer good luck.

Nothing has changed.

Angus Whitson
Man with Two Dogs

JANUARY

Fresh Start

Welcome to January. Christmas celebrations finished on Twelfth Night, the New Year festivities are winding down and the hopes and ambitions for the next twelve months are bright. It's around the end of the first week of this month that the sun begins to rise earlier and the days gradually lengthen.

From the Doyenne's Kitchen

HOT PLOTTY
MY WELCOME TO THE NEW YEAR

This recipe was given to me by my whisky connoisseur father-in-law who lived by the precept that 'there's good whisky and better whisky, never any bad whisky'. We pinched the name from a friend's mulled wine drink and perhaps it's time now to acknowledge our plagiarism. Neither he, nor we, know the meaning of 'plotty'.

1 lemon
Handful of cloves
1 orange
2–3 tablespoons sugar
½ tablespoon of grated cinnamon
½ tablespoon of grated nutmeg
2 bottles red Burgundy
6 tablespoons whisky

Method

Scrub the lemon and stud with cloves. Place on a baking tray and bake in a pre-heated moderate oven for 15–20 minutes.

Scrub the orange and with a potato peeler carefully remove the rind, taking care not to include any of the white pith. Squeeze the juice from the orange.

Add the squeezed orange juice, orange rind, sugar, cinnamon and nutmeg to 1 pint of water in a saucepan.

Bring to the boil then remove from the heat, put on the lid and leave to infuse for 30 minutes.

Strain into a larger saucepan to which you add the wine, whisky and clove-studded lemon.

The perfect balance of ingredients is best achieved by constant trial and error. Add extra sugar and/or whisky to taste. Keep the mixture warm but do not allow it to boil.

And a Happy New Year to one and all!

And now I shall hand you over to that Man and his two dogs.

The Path to Spring

The shortest day, which occurred on 22 December, was noted with approval in this household as we anticipated lengthening daylight hours. But we could all be forgiven for thinking that someone forgot to turn the page in the diary after that. The incessant rain which lasted till after New Year was a dispiriting state of affairs. Thank goodness the cold, brisk weather has arrived and we really can believe that the shortest day is now behind us. The lighter mornings and lengthening evenings are early hints that spring is not far off.

We – the Doyenne and I, that is – were tidying away the Christmas decorations before Twelfth Night. One of our cards contained pressed flowers. A nephew had visited with his girlfriend in the summer and she had picked a bunch of tiny woodland flowers; mounted and laminated they made a charming card and a very personal memory of a happy day.

The cold weather reminds me of a story my Uncle Rob used to tell against himself. He grew up in Edwardian times in the village of Loanhead, outside Edinburgh, when attitudes were more rigid than

3

today. One chilly morning, when aged about eight, he announced to his mother that there was 'a terrible hoor frost outside.' It was quite some time before he understood why his world fell about his ears in a storm of cuffs and wallops and censure!

It's not the best time of year for the Sheba dog, my twelve-year-old Labrador. Sadly, she has arthritis in all four limbs which slows her down in this weather. A pill a day helps, but she looks forward to warm summer days when she can soak up the sun.

We were sharing a welcome glass of sherry with kind friends; a good occupation for a Saturday lunchtime. They have a busy bird table and, to add to our pleasure, a great spotted woodpecker called in for lunch. Shortly afterwards, Mrs GSW joined the party. They are amongst the most elegant of the woodland birds with their crimson, black and white plumage. Both sexes have a patch of crimson feathers beneath their tails but the male is identified by an additional patch of crimson feathers on the crown of his head. I hear woodpeckers in the woods round our house and I intend to investigate a suitable menu to attract them to our bird table.

Night Moves

The dogs get three walks a day. First thing in the

morning. Well, eight hours is a long time for humans to keep it all in and it can't be any easier for a dog. I try to take them for their main walk of the day in the afternoon while it is still light. It isn't always possible at this time of year, so evening walks are sometimes taken in the lanes and tracks around the house by the light of a torch.

And there is always a short walk last thing at night to shed one final tear for Nelson. This is when I hear the foxes barking and, like the Wild Wood in Kenneth Graham's *The Wind in the Willows*, the 'pat-pat-pat of little feet' is all around. Sit down quietly in a wood and listen to the industrious small animals rustling through the dry leaves in their search for food.

That's when the tawny owls tune in. The female calls a short 'kee-wick, kee-wick'. The male's reply is an eerie 'hoooo, hoooo', which sometimes tails off into a quavering shudder of such agonised desolation that I hardly dare close my eyes when I crawl into bed.

I always hope to find evidence of badgers, which are true nocturnal animals, but they are just not common in our part of the world. Some years ago, I saw one dead by the side of the A68 near Otterburn, in the Northumberland National Park. If we had been driving straight home I would have picked it up. When the animals were more plentiful the mask, or face, of the badger was used for the front of sporran pouches. So that badger by the roadside might have been honoured in its death as a very traditional item of traditional Scottish dress.

Although hedgehogs are most active at night it is not uncommon to see them in daylight. Their night-time slaughter on the roads, casualties of speeding cars, proves how many are around, even if we don't often see them. I had a springer spaniel called Stan who regularly retrieved hedgehogs, rolled tight into their defensive ball, but he would refuse to drop them. The only way I could make him release them was to 'clunk' him under the chin and give him a prickly sandwich, which he found most uncomfortable. However often we had this battle, Stan never stopped bringing me these special gifts.

I joined a party which went out with the forest ranger in Glen Doll to hunt for bats. It was a fascinating excursion because I know so little about these night hunters. Using special sound detectors we could hear the bats' ultrasonic calls and our guide identified the various species for us. We also looked at the catch in his moth trap. Some moths have the most vivid colours, which seem quite unnecessary for a life in the dark. They used to just be victims on the windscreen of my car, but now they are part of another world for me to explore.

High and remote, Glen Doll lies beyond Glen Clova, one of the famed Angus glens, and cuts deep into the Eastern Cairngorms and the Cairngorms National Park. Remote Jock's Road is a wild shepherd's track that takes you from the head of Glen Doll all the way to Braemar in Royal Deeside, skirting impressive mountain peaks like Mayar and Dreish, which are Munros and therefore over 3,000 feet high. It's a land of rare alpine plants, red deer, ptarmigan, golden eagles and space to experience wilderness and isolation.

Wealth of Words

The Scotch vernacular has a wealth of expressive, pithy proverbs that condense a reflection on life into a few brief words.

'It's the withered leaf that hings the longest' (some called it the 'sere' leaf) – that one yellow, desiccated leaf which defies all the forces of nature to dislodge it from the branch. Look up at any tree at this time of year and, as likely as not, you'll see that one fragile leaf hanging grimly onto its source of life. In our grandparents' time the old saying described the elderly men and women who outlived their contemporaries, and many younger than them too – wiry and wizened indestructibles, who survived everything that a much harsher life than ours today flung at them.

My mother had another version of the old adage: 'It's the creaking gate that hings the longest'. Despite creaking limbs, rheumatism and sore bones, there are always some who outlast the rest of us. She was ninety-two when she died, so perhaps she knew what she was talking about.

Soon even the enduring, withered leaves will disappear, dislodged by the pressures of new growth and regeneration which tell us that welcome spring

7

will soon brighten our lives. The early snowdrops are in flower with their dainty, nodding heads agreeing with everything you say. It is time for raking up more beech leaves for another bonfire. The pungent smell when you burn them is quite unmistakable and confirms the need to clear up the debris of the past season before we welcome in the new.

In recent months, there has been a great deal of timber felling around the district. It is easy to forget that trees are a crop and that they will be harvested. Taking so long to grow they become part of our landscape and it can be quite confusing to drive round a corner and find a blank space and a new skyline where there used to be a familiar stand of mature trees.

Farmers sowed the winter wheat and oilseed rape in the autumn and it rapidly grew several inches before going into suspended animation during the winter months. The green has provided a splash of colour in contrast to the austere brown of the ploughed fields. A walk round the garden shows plenty of new growth which is well advanced. Buds are appearing on the bushes and shrubs and my favourite, the honeysuckle, has new leaves at each bud.

Not that there isn't time for winter to still give us a skelp (a slap) round the ear for paying too little attention to what is going on round about us. Up till the end of February we shouldn't be surprised at any unexpected deterioration in the weather. As curlers, the Doyenne and I always hope for a really sharp spell of weather which is hard enough, and lasts long enough, to allow a Grand Match to be played.

The game of curling is now an Olympic sport and is regularly screened on television, so shouldn't need any introduction. To be chosen to play in the Grand Match is the pinnacle of every curler's life. Almost as good as winning an Olympic gold medal! The historic competition, or 'bonspiel', takes place between curlers from the north and south of Scotland. From every corner of the country, curlers congregate in their hundreds on the Lake of Menteith near Aberfoyle in West Perthshire, each armed with two curling stones weighing some forty pounds apiece, to play the 'roarin' game' and enjoy the brotherhood of the ice.

First played in 1837, there have been thirty-three Grand Matches played on outdoor ice, the last in 1979 which, to my lasting regret, I could not attend. Global warming and climate change may mean that there will not be another in my lifetime.

The Music Tells You What to Do

Scottish country dancing was something I learned as a child in the time-honoured way by being thrown headlong into Eightsome Reels, Dashing White Sergeants and Strip the Willows.

It all started at a tender age with dancing lessons

in the Park Hotel in Montrose. When I went to prep school in Musselburgh, outside Edinburgh, we all assembled one evening a week in the winter term for lessons from Miss Jean Milligan, the doyenne of the Scottish Country Dance Society, to prepare us for the Christmas dances and parties during the school holidays.

When I brought my own Doyenne back to Angus she found the more complex reels a whirling battlefield of birls and hoochs, which were quite confusing for a girl brought up in Bradford. But she entered into the spirit of things and it wasn't long before she was keeping up with the best of them.

Just after this Christmas past, we and our grandchildren were invited to a reel party by a traditionally-minded grandmother who thought it was time the next generation were introduced to country dancing. I wondered whether, in these days of non-contact dancing, this was going to be 'cool' with the young ones. I needn't have worried. Country dancing is alive and healthy and, from the response we got from the young dancers, has an assured future. This is great, because I like the idea of inviting my granddaughters to join me and lead off a set of the Duke of Perth or a Reel of the 51st Division.

High-Fashion Dogs

Not content with thinking he's an outsize, black West Highland terrier, I fear that Inka may now be thinking he's a cat. He has taken to catching field mice, and brings their limp little bodies into the house, tenderly offering them to the Doyenne. He cannot understand why his gifts attract so much abuse.

In reality, of course, he's a Labrador retriever and you can be sure the original breeders had something more substantial in mind for retrieval than tiny mice. The mice are not quite so irritating as the pebbles which he picks up and 'sooks' like mint imperials before dropping them in dark corners of the house to be 'sooked' up by the Dyson with alarming, rattling explosions.

Activity at the bird table is increasing and a pair of goldfinches have reappeared in the garden. I hear the woodpeckers drumming in the woods round the 'big hoose', and they have started to visit our peanut feeders. They arrive around mid-morning, as does at least one red squirrel.

I can easily waste half an hour and more sitting at the window, drinking my coffee and watching the goings-on. There is an ebb and flow in the feeding habits of the small songbirds. One moment they are mobbing the feeders, then, for no apparent reason and without any apparent signal, they scatter into the surrounding bushes. I never know what it is that panics them because moments later they are back feeding again.

I watch the squirrel coming for the peanuts, running across a piece of rough ground, ever vigilant for danger. With its rapid, jerky movements it looks like a little mechanical toy as it hops and darts about the branches of the tree where I've placed one feeder. When he sits up in his familiar begging pose, with his tail curled up his back, it's small wonder squirrels are such icons of the Scottish countryside.

The dogs were summoned for a photo call. Not a very high-fashion photo call, you understand, but every dog must start somewhere. I thought Inka, at only eight months old, would be an absolute nightmare, wanting to sniff and lick everything, if not worse! I certainly didn't expect him to be so patient for a full hour and a half. He sat and walked to heel to order, as if to the manner born. The outcome of all this photographic activity can be seen at the top of the home page of the 'Man with Two Dogs' website (and now on the cover of this book!).

Macbeth was even more laid-back, but was declared to be 'too clean', the last thing I expected to hear. Obviously, to be a true terrier he should look scruffy and disreputable. We ought to have postponed the photographs for a couple of months until he is due for his next clip. Then he really does look like the 'demented ball of string' the Doyenne once described him as.

Man With Three Dogs

The Doyenne it was who saw him first, lit up in the car headlights. A sad wee figure at the side of the verge, obviously separated from his family and uncertain what to do about it. We turned round and drove back to see if we could catch him and reunite him with his owners.

He hadn't gone much further down the road when we caught up with him. He was a Jack Russell terrier, rather the worse for wear, grubby, disorientated, and separated from his family. He'd lost the wag in his tail and was heading just anywhere – more in desperation than hope. He stopped when the headlights caught him again. It looked as though it would be an easy job to put a lead on him and get him back to the house, but this was when the fun started.

I approached him slowly, making encouraging noises and telling him what a grand wee chap he was. I could get to within about three or four paces of him when his confidence ran out and he trotted off down the road again. Several failures meant a change of tactic, and we went home for Macbeth and Inka.

I set off for where we last saw the runaway, but he had taken to the undergrowth. My two intrepid trackers crashed noisily about as we criss-crossed the area in search of the fugitive. It took well-nigh half an hour to locate him, and he seemed none too pleased to meet our two and was showing them his teeth. I could hardly blame him with Inka capering about like a wild-eyed fanatic.

Having our own dogs with me to distract him made it easier to get in close. He didn't mind a wee tickle behind the ears and, as I slipped the lead over his head, it gave him the familiar sense of security he needed to follow me readily back to the house. From the state of him, and the earthy smell which accompanied him indoors, I suspect he had been down a rabbit hole and been stuck for a while. He was very ready for a bowl of warmed milk and the rest of Macbeth's tin of meat. He was clearly a well cared-for dog and we took him to the Police Station to be taken into custody by the Police dog warden, who would try to locate the owners. And that, we thought, was that.

The following morning, driving away from the house, an anxious figure coming down the road prompted us to stop and ask if he was looking for a dog. Had we seen a Jack Russell? Hadn't we just! Concern turned to delight. There had been tears at home since 'Titch' had gone missing. But this changed everything and the new year was starting on a high note after all. We left the man, mobile phone to ear, calling his wife and daughter to tell them the happy news.

Red Legs

On recent mornings, Macbeth, our West Highland terrier, has been most reluctant to join me for the early run. He pokes his nose out of the door to taste the day, finds nothing to his satisfaction and tries to slip unobtrusively back to the warmth of his bed. In fairness he's just had his regular three-monthly clip – enough undergrowth was snipped off to fill a cushion – so he's experienced a fairly instantaneous climate change. Inka, our black Labrador, greets every morning enthusiastically and is standing at the back door 'paddling' with his front paws on the mat, gasping to be let out.

It's been a grey week; 'coorse', some would say, maybe even 'dreich', to use good Scotch idioms which, I'm glad to say, are still in fairly common use. A friend describes that sort of weather as 'wizened', and I understand what he means.

It put me in mind of being at boarding school on the shores of the Firth of Forth. When it was too wet to even play rugby or hockey we were sent off on seven to ten mile runs in the pouring rain. East Lothian can be a bitter place at this time of year and if you are running in sleety rain and a piercing wind it doesn't matter how hard you run you still get frozen. The only relief was knowing that a deep, hot tub awaited me when I got back, with unlimited hot water to wallow in.

I got to thinking of the fishermen of a hundred years ago, who sailed out of Ferryden and Usan, Auchmithie and Johnshaven, as well as all the other fishing villages up and down this part of the east coast of Scotland. They worked in open sailing boats in all weathers and didn't have the benefit of even being able to keep moving. It was the days when wives still carried their husbands on their backs out to their boats so that they could keep their feet dry!

The boats fishing out of Ferryden had a problem with the tides. The River South Esk flows out of Montrose Basin, past Montrose harbour on the north side and Ferryden on the south, and meets the North Sea at Scurdie Ness Lighthouse. The ebb (outgoing) tide flows down the river and out to sea at a rate of six knots or more, which made entering the river mouth under sail almost impossible at times. The wives kirtled up their skirts and, putting ropes from the bows over their shoulders, walked the boats back up the river to their moorings.

I mentioned this to the Doyenne and she reckoned that compared with these hardy women I had it easy as a schoolboy. She was probably right, as she so often is.

Lead Kindly Light

Now I heard the birds rejoicing in the soft
    returning spring,
Full of pleasure were their motions as they
    spread the glittering wing.
While I gazed I spied a snow-drop's tiny bud
    just bursting through,
It hath borne the winter's darkness with a
    spirit meek and true.

These lines come from a poem entitled 'On the Disappearance of the Snow, and the Sight of the First Snow-drop at Kirkside' dated 1 March 1855 by Alan Stevenson. He was eldest son of Robert Stevenson who built the Bell Rock Lighthouse, twelve miles off the coast from Arbroath, and father of the remarkable four-generation dynasty of Scottish lighthouse engineers. Alan rented Kirkside House near St Cyrus and this is one of several poems he wrote there, originally in Greek, as a diversion in his spare time. People did that sort of thing in those days as an intellectual exercise, just to show that they could.

Alan Stevenson was as prolific a builder of lighthouses as his father. He built the Little Ross Light on the island of that name at the mouth of Kirkcudbright Bay, next door to the Solway Firth. Our son James's in-laws converted the two lighthouse keepers' cottages into a holiday home when they became empty after the light was automated.

Alan's brothers, David and Thomas, built the Scurdie Ness Light at Montrose. Thomas married a Miss Balfour of Mall House, Montrose, and they begat Robert Louis Stevenson, one of Scotland's finest writers, who is reputed to have said that every time he smelt the sea he knew he wasn't far from the work of his family. I grew up just along the road from Mall House at Number 32, The Mall. Sometimes you can scarcely walk out the door without tripping over history.

It's tempting to think that the young Robert Louis visited Kirkside House as a child to play with his cousins. If he ever stayed for a sleepover, he'd have seen his grandfather's winking light on the Bell Rock away to the south as he climbed the stairs with his candle brightening the way to bed.

The Bell Rock has been immortalised in verse more than once. Alexander Balfour (a relation of Miss Balfour of Mall House perhaps?) wrote 'The Legend of the Bell Rock', which is a sentimental epic poem recalling the rock by its old name of the Inchcape Rock. Better known is Robert Southey's ballad 'The Inchcape Bell', which tells how wicked Sir Ralph the Rover 'tore his hair, and cursed himself in his despair' when he foundered on the Inchcape Rock in a storm. He was the author of his own downfall having cut the Inchcape Bell from its moorings on the rock after the local Abbot of Aberbrothock (the old name for Arbroath) had placed it there for the safety of mariners, to warn them of the perils endangering their vessels.

Frozen in Time

In the past I've accused Macbeth of being a fair-weather dog and maybe I've been a bit hard on him, for I sometimes find myself looking for the soft option too. There's a slatted shelf above the stove in the kitchen where I leave my cap, and when it's time to take the dogs out and face the elements I reach for my pre-heated bunnet. Bliss!

Footprints in the frosty grass advancing towards the house and then going away again might have been a warning that someone had been prowling round in the middle of the night. But it had only been me taking the dogs out last thing and then returning. The nights this past week have been magical. The clouds cleared during the evenings and the moon shone out of a star-spangled sky, bouncing the moonlight off the rimey grass. I didn't need the torch – Macbeth showed up like a wee white pudding in the soft light and even black Inka was easy to keep an eye on. Anyway at night-time they don't like the idea of losing touch and always stay close about.

Full moon was on Tuesday and it was the first one of the year. It's like being in another world, with just the dogs and myself for company. There's time to think about the day that's past and what I'm going to do tomorrow. By contrast, Monday morning brought one of the most stunning sunrises I've seen for weeks. There was a half-moon arc of reds and pinks radiating across the whole sky. I called to the Doyenne and we stood outside together just drinking in the beauty of it. But it was over so quickly; we went indoors and when I came out again five minutes later it had all but disappeared.

I got a long letter from a lady who grew up on the farm at Milldens, between Friockheim and Forfar. She's in her eighties now and has been away from Angus for over fifty years, but she told me about life in the country when she was a youngster. She and her brother cycled to nearby Guthrie school. It never closed, even in the depths of snow, and if it was too deep to cycle, they walked. A lady next door to the school made soup during the winter months and the children could buy a bowl of piping hot soup for their lunch for a ha'penny.

As a young woman, and without a car, she biked and walked all over the county, even as far as Blairgowrie, some thirty miles away, riding an old-fashioned push-bike. Each Sunday, her grandfather walked the six miles from Forfar to Milldens and the two of them walked on a further two miles to Dunnichen Church for the service. Then they walked back again. She and a friend cycled to Oathlaw for nights out country dancing and, when the tempo quickened and the dancing got lively, the men used to swing them off their feet!

Her brother guddled trout in the burns (i.e. caught them by hand) and they had them for tea, fried in oatmeal. She helped on the farm, milking the cows and making butter, and she had her own dog too. Six pages of memories she sent me. She lived a busy life, with no time for mischief, and it's little wonder she says she enjoyed life on the farm and in the country so much.

From the Doyenne's Kitchen

BAKED APPLES WITH MINCEMEAT

On evenings and weekends leading up to Christmas our kitchen turns into something resembling a mince pie factory. Despite churning out hundreds of pies for family and friends there's always a little leftover mincemeat in a jar that I find in the middle of January when I can't bear to look at another mince pie until the following Christmas. The leftover is delicious popped into the middle of baked apples.

(Recipe for mincemeat appears in the first *Man With Two Dogs* book.)

Serves 4
4 large Bramley cooking apples
4 dessert spoons mincemeat
4 dessert spoons Demerara sugar
5 fl. ozs water

Method
Wash the apples and remove the stalks and the core, either with an apple corer or a sharp potato peeler, trying not to leave any 'toenails' behind (technical term

for those sharp bits of the core which are sometimes missed)!

Stuff the empty core with the mincemeat and place in a roasting tin.

Sprinkle the apples with Demerara sugar and add the water to the tin.

Bake in a moderate oven at 180 degrees for about 40 minutes until the apples are really tender and the sugar has melted into the water to make a delicious syrup.

Best served with hot custard.

FEBRUARY

Nature Stirs

February is very much a winter month and can be unpredictable, but there is plenty to see and hear in the countryside. Buds are swelling on the trees and shrubs. Snowdrops and catkins on the hazel trees herald the first true hints of spring and the birds are starting to sing and claim their territories as the first steps to attracting a mate.

Porridge in the Drawer

January caught us on the hop a bit, ending as it did with such a hard, cold snap. But I enjoy the clear frosty days; it stirs the blood and it's how I think winter should be.

I used to scorn wearing a cap but, whether it's gaining greater wisdom or losing more hair, I've changed my attitude. Many years ago, I read that we lose up to forty per cent of our body heat through the top of our heads. That's an awful lot to replace in a hurry and I shouldn't like to think I might be contributing to global warming!

Out with the dogs, last thing before bed, the temperature has been well below freezing, and it's been nippy on the tips of the ears. The nights have been very still, and without the background daytime noises the roar of traffic on the A90, even so late on, has been very intrusive. I can follow the sound of Inka's footsteps amongst the dry, frosted leaves when he disappears on his own into the wood. When I wrote about losing sight of him on these night-time walks, kind friends gave him a flashing collar so that I can track him visually as well. It has proved to be a very practical gift.

I've been keeping the bird feeders filled up, which has been much appreciated by the resident bird population. And a second red squirrel has been calling around about elevenses.

The Doyenne was away for several days on granny duty so I had to bothy for myself. I'd been following the correspondence (in the *Dundee Courier*) about bothy loons cooking great pots of porridge each weekend and pouring it into a drawer to cool and be sliced up each morning for breakfast. Thankfully I wasn't driven to that extreme. I'm reasonably competent at looking after myself even if I'm a bit economical with the truth about what I've cooked in the Doyenne's absence.

Before the days of indoor plumbing and electric light, unmarried farm workers (or 'servants', as they were called in the nineteenth century) lived in primitive accommodation. They were lucky if they got a room to themselves and it was not uncommon for several men – 'bothy loons' they were called – to live and sleep in one small room with only a fireplace to do their cooking and sticks of furniture for their comfort. That room was called a 'bothy'. The most basic bothy I ever saw was created in the roof space of a cart shed by roughly flooring the roofing joists and partitioning off part of the space to form a tiny room where the gardener's 'boy' slept.

That cart shed was part of the outhouses of The Kirklands, the former Church of Scotland manse at Logie Pert (between Montrose and Laurencekirk), which was my family home from 1958 until 1994. I have sometimes wondered if the young lad thought himself lucky to have a job that gave him a roof over his head. If he had to endure some of the harsh winters that we experienced when we lived there I can only hope that the milk of human kindness spilled over enough for his master, the minister, to find him warmer accommodation till the spring.

Father was very friendly with the late Jim Scott who farmed Mains of Gallery Farm and lived in the historic Gallery House, which has a fine Jacobean ceiling and is reported to have had 365 windowpanes when it was built in 1680. In the coachman's bothy was a built-in set of deep drawers and Jim would point out one that he said the porridge had been kept in. His daughter, Mrs Elsie Robertson, confirmed this to me when I questioned my own recollection. So when I say I 'had to bothy for myself', I meant I had to cook and 'do' for myself like one of these hardy young farm workers. But I made jolly sure I ate better and lived more comfortably!

We – the dogs and I, that is – took a walk down the banks of the Cruick Water, which flows into the River North Esk just below Stracathro Hospital. The hospital lies between Brechin and Laurencekirk, on the west side of the A90 dual carriageway linking Dundee and Aberdeen.

The sharp weather fairly galvanises Inka and he leapt in and out of the freezing water as if it had been mid-summer. There's some conjecture about the ancestry of Labradors. Despite their name it's unlikely that they originated from Labrador on Canada's east coast. More likely they came from neighbouring Newfoundland where it's thought they were bred as fishermen's dogs because of their thick coats and ability to withstand severe winter conditions – as Inka so clearly demonstrated.

Macbeth, on the other hand, likes his creature comforts. He sees no point in plowtering about a stream-side and adding to his discomfort when his undercarriage is already soaking wet from scrambling amongst the damp grass.

Surviving Winter

The heat starts to go out of the sun around noon at

this time of year. We've had sharp sunny mornings to accompany the arrival of the snow and the hedgerow birds have been busier than usual searching for the constant supply of food they need for survival.

Wildlife in this part of the countryside is well served by the foresight of past landowners who planted miles of beech hedges and great woods of deciduous, broad-leafed trees. The finches and tits, robins and wrens, and bigger songbirds like thrushes and blackbirds have had shelter from the worst of the winds, and there hasn't been so much snow as to completely obliterate the ground. Numerous scrapings and overturned leaves show the birds are having success finding all manner of bugs and beetles. The priority for food makes the birds less cautious about me standing close to them. One robin, in particular, so lost its fear that if I had had some crumbs, I believe it might have come to my hand.

All my dogs have loved the snow. It brought out the puppy in Sheba, and Macbeth believes that because he once was white (and I use the description guardedly) he is completely camouflaged. He used to crouch in the snow and leap out on Sheba like a snarling tiger. She was too considerate to point out that, in fact, he looked like a rather tired white pudding, well past its sell-by date, and that he stuck out like a sore thumb!

This is the time to look for animal and bird tracks. I've found plenty of rabbit tracks despite seeing little evidence of them before. I thought they must have been cleaned out by hunting buzzards. And there seem to be a couple of local hares, which is most encouraging because they have not been a common sight for many years. Cock pheasants leave very distinct tracks with a line in the snow between their footprints, made by their trailing tail feathers, which are longer than those of the hen pheasants.

The star turn amongst our colourful visitors has been a bullfinch, feeding greedily on seeds in the weed and grass heads outside the kitchen window. With his rosy breast feathers he's like the memory of a pink sunset. Lilac, pink and light grey clouds have brightened some wonderful evening skies, and the sun has dazzled out from behind them in a last surge of brilliance before fading into the inky hills.

The Doyenne has made her annual batch of marmalade (recipe to be found in the first book), which will shift like snow off a dyke once the family get to know about it. And grandson James came for a weekend visit which is always welcome. I'm still a better snowballer than he is, but I guess my time is running out. (Postscript – it has!)

Carry on filling your bird tables with food and ensure that your gardens are filled with bird life in the spring. The added pleasure will repay such small effort now many times over.

Woody Tunes

It's been a week of new sightings and sounds. Urgent calls from the Doyenne had me cantering to the other end of the house. A fox had crossed the lawn outside the bedroom window, and a few moments later had trotted back again. I was just in time to see a tawny brush disappearing round the side of the house. If I'd stayed where I was I would likely have seen old Tod running across the back green and escaping out of the garden. La D. was most excited because she had never seen a fox so close to.

I'd come across what I thought were fox droppings on the gravel, but then decided I must be wrong. Several nights previously I was sure I heard two foxes barking at each other and again decided I must be wrong because they were followed by a tremendous amount of irate shouting. Perhaps it was a dog and a fox exchanging insults with each other – but there was no doubt about the shouting!

Despite gloomy weather predictions, the mornings have been mostly bright and sunny. I watched two male woodpeckers squaring up to each other in the bare branches of a plane tree beside the bird table. The morning sun is still quite low in the sky and it caught the vivid scarlet feathers on their rumps as they jostled for territory, flitting in amongst the branches, until one acknowledged defeat and flew back to the wood. Several days later, I heard more woodpeckers drumming in the policies of the big hoose. They were in different trees and their tapping produced two clearly different notes, a bit like a primitive xylophone.

Out with the dogs, last thing before bed, and Inka was taking a great deal of interest in bird droppings below a beech tree on the roadside. I flashed the torch into the branches above and, as I expected, disturbed a roosting cock pheasant. It seemed a very exposed place to spend a cold February night when there was the relative (in pheasant terms) protection and warmth of dense pine trees barely twenty paces inside the wood.

Strung Up

Walking dogs can be hazardous – not for me, but for the dogs. More than once I've watched Macbeth's twitching tail advancing down precipitous banks at the Rocks of Solitude near Edzell, in pursuit of particularly seductive scents. One wrong foot and he'd be whirling into certain oblivion on the rocks below, or into the River North Esk from which I'd fish him out somewhere about Marykirk, several miles downriver. It's the dilemma of deciding whether to holler at him, and distract his attention with possible fearful consequences, or assume that his innate sense of self-preservation will ensure his triumphant return to safer ground. I usually choose a middle road making encouraging noises, and between us we resolve the crisis.

Perhaps I sometimes exaggerate a bit about Macbeth, but there can be no exaggeration of the pickle Inka got himself into. It's happened to other dogs I've owned, and I shan't be surprised if some readers have experienced the same problem when out walking their own dogs.

Until recently, when we have been out walking, Inka has clambered between the lower strands of wire fences, but as he's matured he has started jumping over them. If a dog doesn't clear the fence cleanly there is a danger of a hind leg slipping between the top two strands of wire which can close on the leg trapping it and leaving the dog strung up, with little hope of escape.

This is what happened to Inka and fortunately I was standing beside him and could deal with the matter immediately. A strong, young dog which is frightened and struggling to escape isn't the easiest animal to deal with. The second strand was barbed wire which didn't help matters, and while his flesh was punctured it turned out to be no worse than that.

It's a salutary lesson on the importance of keeping contact with dogs if you take them into the country. It would have been a great deal more traumatic all round if I hadn't been on hand. A man I knew laid his leg along the top strand of wire fences and trained his dog to jump over it. It also prevented the dog ripping its skin (quite a common accident) if the top strand was barbed.

Inka appeared to be going prematurely grey under his chin – aged nine months, for goodness sake! On more careful investigation we think he must have singed off the hair on his lower lip, probably from getting too close to the heat of the wood-burning stove. He's restored to his youthful beauty once more.

The catkins are out on the hazel bushes. 'Lambs tails' they used to be called, and when you see them hanging on the branch it's a most descriptive expression. Y-shaped forked hazel branches were traditionally used by water diviners to trace water courses. I used to think divining was an arcane skill revealed only to hoary old greybeards. But I've tried it with two metal rods with some success – and I'm clean-shaven!

Dog Tails

I hadn't heard of a West Dart water terrier; so called because it was bred beside the River Dart in Devon. Several of its antecedents must have had scant regard for 'the consequences', for it was an agglomeration of a wire-haired terrier, Lhaso apso, Pekinese and poodle! Its most endearing characteristic was a fanatical love of water, from which it could scarcely be kept away. Its owner held it in high regard, saying it looked much like an oily rag. It's dead now, so there's not much more to tell . . .

A fortnight ago, I wrote about the West Dart water terrier whose name, it transpires, was Tigger. I now have a photo of Tigger, and without question he was the archetypal hideous hound. He had an undershot jaw and there's a wild, bite-yer-leg look on his face which says that he preferred to get his own way. His mixed background, resulting from hastily-engaged-in unions, happens all too easily in the dog world unless vigilance on the owners' part is exercised.

My first 'very own' dog, Molly, was a mixture of springer spaniel and collie. With our newly-born daughter Cait asleep in the back of the car, the Doyenne and I drove one wild winter's evening to a farmhouse somewhere near Methlick, in darkest Aberdeenshire, to see some puppies which had been billed as pure-bred spaniel. Doubtless, I thought it would be fun for the Doyenne to have a puppy to look after, just to help pass the time and stop her wearying. I wouldn't get away with that now!

The pure-bred mother was brought into the kitchen trailing three puppies behind her. I know I didn't have much wit then but I remember saying to the breeder that the pups seemed rather long in the leg and they had awful short, pointy ears, not the least like a springer spaniel's.

33

I was assured that their bodies would 'grow into their legs' and the ears would develop normally over the next couple of months. The mother was a couthy animal, which is always a good sign, and we chose the puppy with the waggiest tail. £6 changed hands, the baby's nappy was changed and we were ready for home.

What I didn't know was that a bitch can mate with, and produce puppies, to two dogs – a 'mixed litter' is the veterinary term. The pure-bred puppies had all gone to wiser, more experienced buyers than me, doubtless for a lot more than £6. But Molly turned out to be a nice-natured dog, good in the house and protective of the children. She had an unfortunate predilection for hens, but we'll draw a veil over that.

She was also the toast of the countryside whenever she came on heat. Our neighbours' daughter, Susie, had a miniature dachshund called Monty who was Molly's most ardent and dogged follower. We'll never know whether Monty stood on a straw bale or Molly stood in a ditch, but Monty and nature had their way and Molly produced some strange-looking offspring.

Only one, Thaddeus, survived. He had short legs, a long body and, while quite well disposed towards humans, he was short-tempered and inclined to pick a fight with other dogs – the bigger the better as far as he was concerned. Another bite-yer-leg dog, you might say – especially if you were another dog.

Living Sporrans

There are plenty of jokes about sporrans but it was no joke for a friend who thought he would cut a dash and wear his national costume. When he looked out his sporran he found it had become a breeding ground for several families of unidentified and destructive fly. They had set up home inside the pouch and laid eggs which had hatched, and the resultant maggots were happily munching their way in and out of the fur. Indeed, the sporran looked as though it had taken on a life of its own.

Hearing about this disagreeable experience stirred up the memory of the most exceptional collection of Highland dress accoutrements that I was shown by Pipe Major Bert Barron, who was a doyen of the piping world and piping instructor to the St Andrews University pipe band. Bert was an avid collector of all things Highland and I bought a sporran for each of our sons from him.

In the course of our negotiations he produced from under a bed an ordinary pine box, and when he opened it I could scarcely believe my eyes. There was a waist belt and cross belt (for holding a sword), both with decorated silver buckles; a plaid brooch and dirk, both with socking great Cairngorms; a *sgian dhu* and shoe buckles, all in silver.

But the sporran was the most unusual piece of all. It had a silver link chain and a heavy, ornate cantle (the ornamental arch which decorates the top of the pouch) with long grey hair hanging from it. Bert asked if I could identify the hair, which was fine and soft. My first thought was that it came from a pony's tail. When I felt it again I realised it was human hair. It had been offered by a *cailleach*, an elderly doyenne of her clan, to adorn her chief's sporran. I'd never seen anything like it before, and Bert said it was the only one that he had come across. Engraved in the centre of the cantle was the Mackenzie crest.

Strong Language

A lady in the village shop was complaining about the state of the weather. She'd been out in her garden and been up to her knees in 'dubs' (muddy puddles). That's a fine old Scotch expression that I haven't heard used in everyday speech for a long time. I knew fine she meant that it had been 'gey clarty'.

Sea legs

Macbeth will never be an old sea dog. Inka, on the other hand, shows no fear of the sea and has so much fun when we go down to the beach that if I don't keep an eye on him I believe one day he'll set off to swim to Norway like some homeward-bound Viking.

Tuesday morning dawned like a summer's day and I knew I just had to get down to the sea again. I bundled the bold boys into the car and off we went to Kinnaber and a favourite walk down the bank of the River North Esk on the final stretch of its run to the North Sea.

We sat for a while on the dunes looking across the sand, for the tide had just turned and was starting to come in again. It's very companionable with a black dog on one side and a white one on the other. Macbeth sat there wearing his keenly intelligent look while Inka was panting like a grampus and trying to lick the inside of my ear – which shows how intelligent he is!

You need to make the best of these mornings at this time of year for by lunchtime the heat has started to go out of the day. It was so warm that I'd left my jacket in the car and I could have happily stretched out on the sand and had a snooze, except Inka kept jogging me under the arm with his nose, telling me clearly that it was time for play.

Labradors are water dogs and Inka is just like Sheba, our previous Lab, who drove us near demented whenever we took her to the beach, bringing us sticks to be thrown into the sea, which she would swim out for and retrieve. There was a bit of a swell but Inka plunged into it headlong, cresting the waves like some bygone Hebridean birlinn.

West Highland terriers are underground dogs. They were bred to go down fox holes and flush out the foxes. Macbeth got as far as the water's edge and made it clear that it was quite bad enough getting his feet wet without any of the other nonsense. He was much happier when we turned back up the river bank where he could sniff rabbit holes and think ferocious thoughts.

I watched three dabchicks feeding in slack water on the other side of the river. They are not strong flyers and are much more at home on, or under, the water. They slipped below the surface leaving scarcely a ripple and just when I thought they couldn't stay submerged a moment longer they shot to the surface like released corks.

Back home it was clear that, for once, I'd managed to wear Inka out. He retired to his bed and slept through the afternoon. Macbeth does that most afternoons, of course.

From the Doyenne's Kitchen

Winter suppers are usually hot meals and sometimes my husband makes us pasta with a pasta sauce that he has developed himself. Although it is not strictly my recipe he learnt most of his cooking skills from me (memories of turmoil, trauma and tantrums!) so, with my blessing, he includes it here.

ANGUS'S GENEROUS PASTA SAUCE

Serves 2

Method

Into a pot with a tablespoon of sunflower oil (or olive) to sweat at lowest heat:
2 onions, roughly chopped (could be leeks if no onions)
2 cloves of garlic chopped small (crushed if preferred)

Add: 3 rashers of streaky bacon cut into medium cubes
6 or 8 sliced mushrooms

Fry gently, with a lid on, for about 5 minutes to release the flavours.

Add: a generous teaspoon of green pesto
tin of peeled, chopped tomatoes
salt and freshly ground pepper
3 squirts of tomato purée
a generous handful of pine nuts
a generous handful of raisins

For added flavour I have used any of the following ingredients – chopped savoury sausage, cashew nuts, olives and flaked almonds. You are limited by your own imagination what extras you use.

Also crème fraiche, sour cream and Greek yoghurt (individually, not all together!) mixed in about 5 minutes before serving so as to be heated through.

Put lid back on and leave to cook on a low heat until ready to serve (about 20 minutes), stirring occasionally to avoid sauce sticking to the bottom of the pot.

Grate a generous amount of fresh Parmesan cheese for sprinkling over the sauce when serving.

The pasta – follow the manufacturer's instructions on the packet. My only advice is, cook it for the longer of the two usually-recommended times. To add to the total experience, once the pasta is cooked *al dente* drizzle a little oil over it, put the lid on the pan and shake briskly to coat the pasta.

Red wine – I don't put wine in the sauce but a glass, or better still two, of good Rioja rounds off a very tasty supper.

MARCH

First Awakening

The last of the geese are crying farewell and flying off on the long return journey to their northern breeding grounds. Our native birds are taking on their mating colours. Daffodils and primroses have replaced the snowdrops and crows celebrate their special Sunday holiday.

Big Black Crow

1 March is always St David's Day, an important day for Wales. But the first Sunday in March is always 'Crow Sunday', an important day for crows in Scotland; the day, traditionally, when crows start to build their nests.

The crow family, generally, gets a pretty bad press which is not altogether justified. Crows or, more properly, carrion crows do indeed feed on carrion and in this respect carry out a useful function. Some of their other habits, such as their reputation for pecking the eyes out of newborn lambs and other weak and defenceless animals, might appear cruel, but in reality are the birds' natural instincts. As a youngster I was told that crows and rooks don't have strong talons like hawks to hold their prey, so they blind it to prevent its escape and give them time to despatch it. It's nature's old story of the survival of the fittest.

Crows are notorious egg thieves and can wreak devastation on bird's eggs in springtime. Ornithologists and gamekeepers tell of marking out the sites of ground-nesting birds such as grouse with stakes, to make future location and study easier, and several days later finding that the crows had worked out what the stakes were for and cleaned out all the eggs. So they are highly intelligent and efficient in their endless pursuit of food.

I've heard stories that during the Second World War newly-fledged rooks were shot, sent to top London restaurants and passed off as grouse. Around about May time my mother used the breasts of fledgling rooks to make my father rooky pie. (Another recipe in the first book.) In the first flush of marriage, the Doyenne tried her hand at this delicacy, but she tried it only once and has since firmly declined. Rooks have a mainly vegetable-based diet of grain, fruit and seeds, with only occasional carrion, so its flesh is much more palatable than crow meat.

Jackdaws are the little rascals of the crow family, reputed to be attracted to anything that is shiny. There are stories, especially in children's literature, of spoons and jewellery and other bright objects being found in their nests, but I've never actually seen this myself.

My raven story is about a raven in Edinburgh

Zoo. Aged about five I was held up to its cage and told specifically not to poke my fingers through the wire netting. So of course I did. I got a severe nip for my troubles and was carted off, amidst stern parental admonitions, bawling like a stirk and full of self-pity.

I haven't heard the expression for a long time, but people used to say, 'I was rooked,' meaning 'I was cheated.' 'Crow's feet' around the eyes are something no girl wants and 'old crow' is one of the unkindest terms of derision. So the birds' ill-starred reputations have been absorbed into our everyday language.

This article appeared in the paper on Saturday, 1 March, so inevitably the first Sunday of the month was the following day, and I finished the piece with: 'Keep a sharp lookout tomorrow. If you see crows flying about with twigs in their beaks you'll know that Crow Sunday isn't an old wives tale.'

Winter's Demise

Brown predominates in the countryside at this time of the agricultural cycle. The last of the fields are being ploughed and the landscape is a countryside-in-waiting for conditions to improve and sowing to start. Having said that, I've passed several fields ploughed into the familiar arrow-straight ridges indicating that early potatoes have already been planted. The brown is broken up by green patches of winter barley and oilseed rape, which were sown in the back end of last year. They grow a couple of inches before winter sets in and then go into a sort of agricultural hibernation until the weather warms up in the spring and growth resumes.

The pattern of the seasons is on the turn. The geese are leaving us and returning to their summer nesting grounds. Although some greylag nest in the Outer Hebrides, most fly north to Iceland. Pink-footed geese nest even further away in Greenland, and both species return to Scotland at the end of their breeding season when the winter temperatures have fallen so low there is no food for them.

As the snowdrops wither they are replaced by the daffodils with their own bonny display of colour. The mornings are drawing out and the bird table starts to get busy at about half past six. The red squirrel, which was absent for several weeks when the frost was bad, now calls most mornings for the peanuts. The woodpecker hasn't put in an appearance for several months, so we look forward to his (it usually seemed to be the male bird with the crimson patch of feathers on the nape of his head) visits starting again.

A buzzard lifted from the road verge in front of the car. It was feeding on a cock pheasant which could have been knocked down by an earlier passing car. The pheasant's breast had been neatly filleted by the buzzard and its innards gralloched (a deer stalking term for disembowelling), quite possibly helped by scavenging crows. I took the dogs that way the following afternoon and the pheasant's clean-picked carcass was plainly visible.

The morning after that the carcass had disappeared leaving only a circle of feathers. I suspect a fox had picked it up during the night, but there would have been pretty short commons left for it to feed on. Grains of barley which had spilled out of the pheasant's crop had also all disappeared, possibly to hungry mice. Nature makes sure nothing is wasted in the daily competition for survival.

At twenty-three minutes to six this morning, as dawn broke, I was roused by another cock pheasant which 'clokked' just the once, unlike another cock bird which crowed three times!

Slippery Customers

Eels have a special place in the dark recesses of the Scottish psyche. Why and when we developed a distaste for eating them is very much a mystery.

It can't always have been so because there are still working eel traps and enough evidence of old ones in the county of Angus alone, to make it clear that eels were an important item of diet at one time.

I spent an informative morning at Milldens Mill, between Friockheim and Forfar, being shown over the historic, and still working, meal mill, and the eel trap which relies on the mill lade to provide its harvest of eels.

Eel traps benefit from simplicity for their effectiveness. The Milldens trap is nothing more than a large, square box lined with quarried stone slabs. It has an inlet from the mill lade, and an outlet to carry away the water. The Lunan Water, which feeds the mill lade that powers the mill, flows eastwards to the sea from Rescobie Loch (lying east of Forfar), through Balgavies (pronounced Balguys) Loch and down to Lunan Bay, between Montrose and Arbroath.

The eels are born in the Sargasso Sea, somewhere south of Bermuda. They come to Scotland as elvers, and feed and grow in our streams, ditches and lochs until they are mature. Then, like our salmon which return to their mother rivers to spawn, instinct tells the adult eels that it's time to make the enormous journey back to the Sargasso, to start the whole mysterious reproductive cycle all over again.

Migration down traditional waterways like Lunan Water occurs in September and October. Best catches are made on moonless nights, when river levels are rising and the water is turbid and clouded. These conditions may provide some sort of natural protection to help hide the migrant fish from otters which, after man, are their worst predator. A series of grills controls the eels' progress along the mill lade until the only way forward is through a pipe from the lade into the eel trap, from which there is no escape.

Up until the 1960s and, to a lesser extent, the 1970s, eels were caught and smoked locally, and I recall them fondly as a particularly delicious meal. But most went by train to Billingsgate Fish Market in London or to the Continent. Transport became much more difficult in the mid-1960s when Dr Beeching's disastrous report – 'The Reshaping of British Railways' – closed many small rural railway stations and cut thousands of miles of the railway network on cost and efficiency grounds. Up until then the catch from Milldens had gone to Billingsgate from neighbouring Aldbar Station, until it too became a Beeching victim. Thereafter, the eels were transported live in water in specially tanked lorries. Declining catches mean that now it is more difficult to find regular markets.

So what is it about eels that makes our Celtic fantasies writhe? They are long, sinuous and serpent-like. Pick one up and it will wrap its tail and body round your hand and wrist like a tentacle. Worse still, they have slippery, slimy skins and can travel overland, usually during the uncertain hours of darkness. They surely can't be fish because they can survive out of water, nor can they be snakes which have reassuringly dry skins.

Maybe there's something about them of Old Nick himself that gives us the creeps.

Egg-cellent

Living in the country means being aware of agricultural smells. Round here it's slurry-spraying time. Slurry, quite simply, is liquid fertiliser derived from the liquid and semi-solid waste of cattle and pigs, which is spread on fields – and it has a distinctive pong. It may not be altogether accurate to say that we've been serenaded by the smell of slurry in recent days, but the air round here has sure been humming.

Brown, speckled eggs are tastier than the wersh-looking white ones – or so they say. And fresh laid eggs are tastier than older ones. That's what grannies tell their grandchildren, and grandchildren believe everything their grannies say. Maybe grannies know a thing or two – I certainly know one who says she does!

Grandchildren Cecily and Fergus arrived to visit with half a dozen of the brownest eggs I've seen in a long time, laid by their own hens and collected only that morning. They were special, truly free-range, so they were kept separate from the bought ones. The following morning, for Sunday breakfast, the Doyenne and I sat down to brown boiled eggs and toast.

It's immaterial what the reality is, but do you know what – those eggs tasted absolutely delicious. They had deep yellow, almost orange yolks and were so fresh that the one I boiled for the Doyenne was underdone. I don't know what the science of it is, but the Doyenne tells me that a really fresh egg takes longer to boil than an older one. She thinks it may have something to do with the consistency of the egg white. Of course, it's too late to do anything about it once you've chopped the top off, as she had, but I popped my own egg back in the boiling water for a couple more minutes. So even if we were just kidding ourselves and believing our own grannies' romancing, it didn't matter – we felt a lot better after breakfast.

Fergus also brought his all-in-one suit which zips up all round him, and once he's got his wellies on he's supposed to be waterproof. I'm afraid the manufacturers didn't do their product research thoroughly enough and failed to take Fergus into account. By the time he had run half a mile down the burn and jumped in all the puddles it was obvious why daughter-in-law Kate had come armed with a complete change of clothing for him. Happiness comes in many forms, but for Fergus it means being soaked to the skin and wanting to do it all over again after the change into dry clothes.

It was 1977, more than thirty years now, since I gave up law and ceased to be a solicitor. But in the ten years that I was in practice – do solicitors always just practise and never actually do it for real? – I would sometimes call on country clients. Once in a while, when I left, I would find half a dozen or a dozen eggs lying on the passenger seat of the car, wrapped in a brown paper bag which had been saved and recycled from the previous week's messages. I wonder how many solicitors are treated to that little compliment these days.

Grace

Some things fair take your breath away. I was hearing about a London dog owner who has a Labrador, like Inka, and before the dog is allowed indoors after a walk the owner brings out a bowl of water and a towel and ceremoniously washes and dries the dog's feet. 'Toonser dogs!' growled an elderly country vet when he heard the story.

However much the Doyenne grumbles about our two bold boys trailing dubs and gutters into the kitchen, we've only rarely had to go the length of washing them down before we let them in. Otherwise we'd never be off our knees for mollycoddling dogs.

This set off a train of thought about the foot washings and blackenings which are traditionally a part of

Scottish pre-wedding celebrations, with the bride and groom as victims of the hilarity and junketing. They are customs to signify the couple's farewell to their single state and set them on the road to married bliss.

It's been a while since I saw a girl, or a young man, being taken round the town, face blackened with soot, or sometimes something even worse. Girls did indeed, traditionally, have their feet washed in a tub, and grooms had their feet smeared, or 'blackened', with soot and ashes. The two customs seem to have merged into one ritual, with the young lads coming off worse, as you might expect.

Face blackened, wearing their best 'auld claes' and trailing ribbons, girls were led up the High Street arm in arm with a friend on each side, and sometimes a tail of friends following on behind. Often someone rang a handbell to draw attention to the bride-to-be, and they sang and laughed their way to deliver her for her last night at the family home. Drink-fuelled daftness usually meant the groom had a harder time. I've seen young men stripped to their underwear, clarted with engine grease and tied up in the back of a pickup truck, being driven round the town, which must test their sense of humour.

Still on old rituals – I was given the following grace by Rev. John Forbes who was the one-time Minister of the Glens.

> *Holy, holy, roond the table*
> *Eat as muckle as you are able.*

> *Holy, holy, pooch nane*
> *Holy, holy, Amen.*

I thought it must be a completely unique blessing, but looking through an elderly, faded miscellany entitled *Lang Strang – being a Mixter-Maxter of Old Rhymes, Games etc.* printed by The Forfar Press, I found the following:

> *Gracious Peter, look ower the table,*
> *Eat as much as you are able –*
> *Eat plenty, pouch nane –*
> *Gracious Peter, Amen.*

'Pooch' or 'pouch nane' is an exhortation not to pinch any of the table cutlery and is accompanied by theatrical actions of secreting a spoon in a pocket, or in my case, in my sporran.

Dog Talk

'Okay, you'll get a cuddle when I get back,' called the husband on his way out. 'What was that, dear?' responded the wife. 'Nothing, dear,' replied the husband, 'just talking to the dogs.'

Domesticated Birds

I watched him strolling confidently along the avenue between the high beeches. The mid-morning sun, shining through the bare branches, lit up his rich chestnut and golden brown bodywork and his bottle-green head. He was gorgeous and he knew it. He stopped for a moment to ruffle his feathers, no doubt the pheasant equivalent of checking that his tie was still perfectly knotted and that just the right amount of handkerchief was showing from his breast pocket.

He calls most days to pick at the seeds below the bird table that the tits and the finches have discarded, so he's a useful visitor. His spring plumage is very grand. As is his royal progress; fastidiously picking up his feet with each step and drawing the claws into a pointed bunch, then splaying them out again as he rather primly prepares to place them on the ground, as if fearing to tread in something quite revolting. The bird table is right outside the kitchen window so I have a front row seat to watch the action.

Unlike the woodpeckers, which are very proprietorial about the feeders when they call, the pheasant is happy to share with the robins and sparrows. The slightly curved beak gives him a supercilious look. I gave a tap on the window and he turned his basilisk eye, sitting in its red cheek wattle and ringed with tiny gold feathers, on me as if to say, 'I'll take your question after lunch, young man.'

Although they are truly wild birds, pheasants will quickly accept human company, especially when food is on offer. Friends had a daily morning visit from a cock pheasant named Jocky, which tapped on the kitchen window with his beak, signalling that it was time for the children to leave their own breakfast and come out and serve him his. Percy (another cock pheasant), on the other hand, preferred the walled garden. Sooty, an experienced hunting cat when outside of it, regarded everything within the walled garden as family, and he and Percy were often seen there, sitting side-by-side in harmonious compatibility.

Snoozing gently in the sunshine, the Master of the Hoose was awoken by an insistent pecking at his leg – Percy was peckish! Being of kindly disposition the M-o-H went indoors by the French windows and through the dining room, dogged – in a manner of speaking – every step of the way by Percy, to the utility room where the bird food was kept and where Percy could be served lunch in style.

This familiarity with humans proved fatal for Jocky who met an untimely end, and history does not say whether Percy died of contented old age. But the two stories show how wild birds will readily exploit any opportunities that make it easier to forage for food.

The M-o-H assures me Percy would be thrilled to have been immortalised in this way.

Harsh Reality

From time to time friends contact me with their own countryside stories. Arthur Grewar has lived in the country and worked on the land all his life, finishing as farm grieve on a farm outside Brechin. 'Grieve' is one of those wonderfully inclusive Scottish terms which never quite pins down the totality of its substance, but everyone understands its meaning. It's not quite a manager, nor foreman or estate factor – perhaps 'person in responsibility' best sums it up.

Arthur phoned me with a story of maternal pluckiness that takes some beating. He was harrowing a field, breaking up the ground in preparation for ploughing, and two very young leverets, no bigger than the size of his fist, ran out from beneath his tractor wheels. Almost immediately a carrion crow and a buzzard appeared, obviously intent on taking the two young hares. The mother hare rose up on her hind legs and attacked both birds with such ferocity that she drove them off. In a lifetime on the land, Arthur said, he had never seen anything so courageous.

Not so lucky was another leveret. It must have been practically newborn because a crow was able to pick it up and carry it off in its beak. Both parent hares were in hot pursuit, frantically leaping into the air, trying to force the bird to drop their baby. They succeeded, but the crow caught its prey again and flew off with it to a nearby wood.

T-Names

I've been investigating the origin of 'Swankie's doo', which I came across in a guide to old Scottish bird names. It translates as 'Swankie's pigeon', but is a local T-name or 'nickname' for a seagull, in the same way as the expression 'Lammermuir lion' is a facetious name for a sheep; the Lammermuir Hills in the Scottish Borders being notable sheep country.

They used to say that 'cod and corn dinna gang the-gither', meaning that the fisherfolk and farmers don't associate with each other. The fishing communities of north-east Scotland developed and lived in some isolation from the broader community, and there was frequently animosity between the two that led to the fishermen being marginalised and cut off socially from their neighbours. Sometimes they were the creators of their own destiny. I've heard stories of Montrose lads trying to court Ferryden lasses and being stoned out of the village for their pains.

Consequently, the fishing communities became very close-knit and inward looking, seldom marrying out-with their own communities and certainly only marry-ing their own kind, for theirs was a hard and dangerous life and it was rare for an inland girl to want to marry into it. The result was that there were few surnames in proportion to the total population of any village. So, for instance, if your surname was West, Paton, Pert or Coull you came from the village of Ferryden, because these surnames predominated in Ferryden and nowhere else.

Likewise, Auchmithie and Arbroath fisherfolk were readily identified by the surnames Spink, Cargill and Swankie. To get to the root of why someone called Swankie should have been associated with a pigeon that was really a seagull, I started at Arbroath and called fish merchant, Brian Swankie, to see what he knew about the expression. While he acknowledged that it is well known around Arbroath he told me that there is no family tradition attached to it.

So I called Bob Spink who is reputed to have an encyclopaedic knowledge of Arbroath and its fishing heritage. Likewise, he had grown up with the name but had no idea how it came into the local parlance. We agreed that it was sad to see the old expressions and language disappearing because they add such colour to conversation.

I was most interested, therefore, to get a letter from Alastair Cownie of Arbroath with a possible explanation. In the 1920s the fish-buying business of Swankie and Smith operated at the 'Fit o' the Toon', i.e. at the foot of the town, beside the harbour. As Alastair explained, 'Betsy Swankie was the boss lady in the partnership and nothing happened in the fish trade without her say-so'. She sounds to have been a pretty colourful character – the Doyenne of the Arbroath fish trade, you might say!

In those days, when the fishermen landed their catch at the quay a bell-ringer went round the harbour streets to warn buyers that the fish sales would shortly be starting. Her influence in the fish market and on fish prices was such that the fishermen would ask the auctioneer to wait until Betsy arrived before he started selling. Since Betsy was such a force within the fish trade it was reckoned that the seagulls must surely belong to her too – hence the expression. She must have prospered, for she could afford a car with a driver, which would have been fairly unusual for a woman then.

Strong women have always emerged from time to time, perhaps no more so than in the Scottish east coast fishing communities. There are stories from the end of the nineteenth century about the widow who owned the Esk Hotel in Ferryden, which at that time was a busy fishing village on the other side of the River South Esk from Montrose. As well as selling them liquor, she loaned money to the fishermen and became wealthy enough to own a carriage and pair, and be driven around the village and on shopping expeditions into Montrose.

We have a 'first' success story from the garden. A pair of long-tailed tits have appeared and are feeding at the bird table. Their tails are about half as long again as their roly-poly bodies, hence their name. Their distinctive domed nest with an entrance hole near the top has led to them sometimes being called 'bottle tits' by country folk.

Come to the Ceilidh

Springers, or early run spring salmon are in the Rivers

North and South Esk on the final leg of their annual passage upriver to the headwaters of the river systems to spawn. As I walked with the dogs down the North Esk from the Rocks of Solitude towards the Gannochy Bridge I hoped I might see at least one, leaping out of the water in its exuberance at being back in its mother stream.

The gorge narrows at The Loups and white water was boiling through the constricted gap. When the river is in spate and the force of the water is too great for them to swim up the main stream, the salmon use the fish ladder cut into the river bank. It was hacked out of solid rock by hand and is a simple channel rising by a series of shallow steps. The diversion reduces the water's speed of flow allowing the fish to swim to the next stage of their journey.

A couple of canoes lay beside the path and two figures standing on the rocks below turned out to be members of Edinburgh University Canoe Club, who were enjoying a day's exciting water sport. Safety is obviously paramount as was evident from their red protective helmets and the buoyancy belts around their middles. These two were the support team for three colleagues who still had to negotiate the falls. One, a student nurse, had secured herself with a rope to an outcrop of rock. Her companion had a throw line to use if any of the other three overturned in the wild water and went under. If he was a bit too energetic when he threw the rope and in danger of toppling into the water himself, the lassie was supposed to hang onto straps on his back and save him. I couldn't help thinking that a reversal of responsibility might have been fairer!

They'd had a great day – a couple had indeed flipped into the water, but their wet suits had kept them insulated from the worst of the cold and they looked forward to coming back again for another dookin!

Two dozen like-minded souls, which included the Doyenne and myself, met last weekend to sing songs and tell stories, very much in the spirit of the traditional Scottish ceilidh. At least half the company sang a song or recited a poem or monologue remembered from childhood, and the evening was full of laughter and humour. Musical accompaniment was provided by our hostess on the squeeze box and the Doyenne on the piano.

Most participants professed to being a little nervous at having to perform publicly, but we all surprised ourselves at how well we did. In any event the standard was very high and we were a sympathetic audience and readily applauded every piece. To keep up our strength a delicious supper was provided which we ate in stages during intervals in the entertainment.

We've got used to packaged entertainment on the telly, but the evening showed how much latent talent we all have when we cast off our inhibitions and share it with kindred spirits.

Female Power

Past Tigerton (pronounced Tiggerton), where the road branches left to Edzell and right towards Little Brechin, you cross a burn called the Buttery Burn, as I have just found out from looking at the map. In the corner of the field beside the bridge over the stream I watched a heron and a buzzard for a few moments. Nothing especially odd about two such birds being in the same field, except there was scarcely twenty feet between them and I hadn't seen that before.

The buzzard was mantling its wings, flapping them as if it would fly at the heron and attack it. Perhaps the heron had caught a frog or an eel in the burn and the buzzard hoped it could unsettle it enough to make it disgorge its meal, which the buzzard would gobble up. I'll never know, for the heron lost its nerve and flew off. The buzzard gave me a dirty look for interfering in its dinner arrangements and flew off too, in a huff.

I carried on to Milldens Mill (earlier the subject of eel traps) to see Stephen Sampson who has compiled a history of the mill and the district. I was delivering a copy of a letter I'd received from a lady who grew up on his farm eighty years ago. On the other side of the Lunan Water, opposite the mill, is an old cottage and croft. Stephen was visited a while back by a man who was born in the cottage, and who told him that his father had ploughed his small fields with a single furrow, a one-way plough yoked to an old shire horse and a bullock.

Unusual perhaps, but not unprecedented I'm sure. It couldn't compare with Stephen's story of holidaying in the Pyrenees forty years ago. He watched a farmer working his land, and the plough was drawn by a bullock and a young woman!

Cat in the Attic

Last Tuesday dawned bright and sunny and it seemed just the morning to drive up the coast to Inverbervie.

Bervie, as it is better known locally, is one of the early Scottish Royal Burghs and received its charter from King David II in gratitude for assistance he received from the villagers – 'kindly received' was the expression used – when his ship was wrecked on rocks known as Craig David. Several cottages in the village were roofed with timbers salvaged from the wreck. There's a story that one of them is haunted by the ship's cat which drowned when the king's ship foundered. It must have retained a supernatural connection with the wrecked ship for whenever the weather is stormy it can be heard mewing and crying in the attic space.

I parked down by the shingle beach but wasn't tempted to get out of the car. The weather had turned nasty and it was cold and sleeting. I took my lead from Macbeth and decided to be a fair-weather walker. I listened to the constant rumble of the pebbles sliding up and down the beach with the movement of the waves. Several hundred years ago there was a harbour here, but the sea and the shingle closed up its entrance and the fishermen moved a couple of miles down the coast to Gourdon.

Gurdon, as it is pronounced locally, was the last fishing village on the east coast, and possibly anywhere in Scotland, to catch fish commercially with hand lines (i.e. hand-hauled fishing lines). Fishermen from the fishing communities married fishermen's daughters who were born into the lifestyle and had grown up used to 'sheelin and baitin' the lines. It was a wearisome and dirty job shelling mussels harvested from Montrose Basin, and baiting 1,200 hooks on a long line that paradoxically was called a 'sma' (small) line'.

It was always said that line-caught haddock was firmer fleshed and tasted sweeter than fish caught in the great purse and seine nets, for those fish were dragged through the sea and drowned (which may seem another contradiction). When I brought the Doyenne home as a bride to Logie Pert she had never eaten line-caught fish and she bought it in preference to any other. Sadly, from the consumers' point of view, the line fishing stopped altogether early in the 1990s because the wives could no longer be persuaded to carry on the 'sheelin and baitin' – hardly surprising, really!

Last stop was Johnshaven, another of the local fishing villages which I'm very fond of and where, for a short time, I kept a boat. Lobster pots, or creels, were piled up on the side of the harbour in 'fleets' –

traditionally roped together in lines of twenty. I passed the time of day with a retired builder who was restoring a boat which has been laid up for several years. He told me he'd have her in the water again within a couple of months and he'll keep her down at Ferryden opposite Montrose harbour. I'll be looking out for her.

From the Doyenne's Kitchen

SPRING RHUBARB

Young rhubarb is quite delicious and, coming from Yorkshire, you could say I was brought up on 'rhubub' as my Father called it. (My mother-in-law thought it was inedible as it is so acidic.) It's so versatile: good in pies, crumbles and fools; baked or stewed; made into jam with ginger; even rhubarb and venison sausages! I have two favourites. One is a compote of rhubarb with bananas and the other is a fudge crumble.

RHUBARB AND BANANA COMPOTE

1 lb rhubarb
6oz caster sugar
Juice of one orange
3 bananas

Method

Wipe and trim the rhubarb stalks and cut into 1 inch pieces. Place in an ovenproof dish with the sugar and orange juice. Cover and bake for 35 minutes in a medium oven. Take out and leave to stand for about 10 minutes.

Slice the bananas into 'pennies' and place in a serving dish. Pour over the hot rhubarb and the juices. Leave to cool then chill in the fridge. Serve with cream or ice cream.

RHUBARB FUDGE CRUMBLE

This has the same ingredients without the bananas. Cook the rhubarb the same way, and make a crumble with digestive biscuits.

4 oz butter
4 oz Demerara sugar
6 oz digestive biscuits crushed into crumbs
1 rounded teaspoon cinnamon

Method

Melt the butter in a pan, stir in the digestive crumbs, sugar and cinnamon and cook for 5 minutes, stirring from time to time. Spoon the mixture over the surface of the cooled, cooked rhubarb and bake in the oven at 200 degrees Celsius or gas mark 6 for 15–20 minutes.

APRIL

Green Shoots of Spring

*The countryside is alive with birdsong. Look for birds –
beaks full of nesting material – winging to and from their
nest sites. Expect to see the first swallows and early hatches
of mallard ducklings, and hear the first cuckoo. A time for
bumble bees, frogspawn, bluebells, blossom and, if you are
lucky, cowslips.*

What a Din!

Peace you can expect up the glen, but quiet is a harder
commodity to come by. The wildlife community is quite
different from the one we see outside our kitchen window at home, as was evident from the clatter of noise
that woke us every morning.

The small songbirds worked hard to make themselves
heard above the racket of the bigger birds: squalling
seagulls; 'chacking' jackdaws; the piping oyster catchers' 'kleep, kleep' calls as they flashed across the house;
whaups (the old Scottish name for curlews) with their

bubbling call sounding like a woody stop on an organ console; the cockerel at the farm next door; haughty cock pheasants parading their grandeur at each other; and gentle cushie doos, or wood pigeons, adding a softer note to the new day's dawn chorus.

The Doyenne and I had joined daughter Cait and her family and a bourach of their friends and children for a long Easter weekend at Tarfside, the village at the head of Glen Esk, the most northern and, some say, the most loveliest of the Angus glens. The glen is a great favourite of the Whitson family, and Cait and her husband were reviving family holidays, spent up there for thirteen years on the trot during the Easter school breaks. I think the Doyenne and I were included to provide a steadying influence to the event!

We had a wonderful away-from-it-all time, with lots of good company and food. The youngsters had freedom and fresh air. One of the guests played the bagpipes and in the evenings we danced reels. On Saturday night more friends tipped up for supper and dancing, and when darkness fell the owls hollered in protest.

Treasure Trove

The Doyenne often remarks on my reluctance to throw anything out. We'd been clearing the barn of 'treasures' which hadn't been used, or even looked at, for years. It was time to be ruthless – or so said the Doyenne – but the moment her back was turned I was squirrelling them away in corners we'd already checked through.

I opened a box full of knitting needles and Herdwick sheep's wool, which was an echo from the Doyenne's childhood growing up in Yorkshire. That box hadn't been opened since long before we left The Kirklands, our family home for nearly thirty years. I doubt if the Doyenne had wielded a knitting needle in anger since about 1993, when she started to knit me a tank top jersey. I still await the finished article. I suppose there's been a minor reconfiguration of my silhouette since then, but if she is still inclined to complete it perhaps she should measure our oldest grandson James for it because, at the rate he grows, in a short while he'll be much the same size as I was a long while ago! (Update: at the time of publishing James has overtaken me, so we'd best go to next grandson down – Alfie.)

Amongst the knitting needles was a blue painted L-shaped rod. It was one of a pair of divining (or dousing) rods given me by the late Captain Mel Evans of Clearbank Farm, near Brechin. He was an original character and entertaining company, for he had no reverence for meaningless authority and expressed his opinions pithily.

He was interested in the earth's energy lines and had the ability to make the rods respond to them. He taught me how to use the rods and I was able to trace the line of the old iron pipe for the water supply to The Kirklands where I had lost it in the garden. I also traced the old drainage system in the steading outbuildings.

Grass cutting is upon us once more. I don't know why we do it – we just encourage it to grow again.

Disbelief

I hardly believed it when I got a phone call to say that a hoopoe was feeding in a field near Edzell. I've always believed them to be southern French and Mediterranean birds which are occasional summer migrants to the warm south of England. But investigation bears out that occasionally they get blown off course, and there are previous records of sightings in our colder northern parts.

I was five times down to the field hoping to catch a sight of the hoopoe, but all I saw was a pair of teal and a red-legged partridge standing guard about twenty yards down a ditch-side. There's likely a hen bird sitting on eggs nearby and the cock was drawing my attention, and the potential danger I represented, away from the nest.

There's nothing new. Mr Edward McBay from John-shaven sent me a cutting from the *Courier* of September 1969 reporting on the hoopoe he saw 'perched on a dyke at the west end of the village'. It was accompanied by a letter from Colin Gibson who was my predecessor on the *Courier* and wrote his Nature Diary for the paper for more than forty years. Colin mentions hoopoe sightings at Carnoustie and other parts of the county of Angus. He comments that the one seen by Mr McBay must surely have spent some time even further north of Johnshaven and that it was on its journey back south. There are no records of hoopoes nesting in Britain, but September, when this bird was sighted, does seem late in the year for such an exotic bird to have been seen so far north.

Sub-Tenant

Interesting observations on the countryside and wildlife have come my way. An unusual story is of a nest with six mallard eggs in it as well as a couple of pheasant eggs. I suspect the pheasant has been the likely 'cuckoo in the nest', but it's all academic now because a fox has found the nest and consumed the eggs.

A reader e-mailed to say that the swallows had arrived at her house and she wondered how this would affect the pair of wrens that were squatters in one of last year's swallows' nests. Did they 'hot nest' she queried, in the same way we humans 'hot bed'? It's an intriguing thought that hadn't occurred to me. So far as the wrens are concerned I would think there would be no question of 'hot nesting'. Wrens are pugnacious little birds, quite ready to see off any swallows thinking of returning to, or sharing, last year's family home.

Cuckoos can't be said to 'hot nest' either. They lay one egg in up to about a dozen host nests – it's called 'brood parasitism' – and that's the extent of their parental efforts as they leave the unsuspecting, and eventually confused, host birds to hatch and rear their offspring.

Could last week's story about the duck's nest with pheasant eggs in it be nearer to 'hot nesting' – i.e. two birds taking turns to incubate two sets of eggs? That doesn't seem likely either. Could the duck have deserted her nest? Mallard ducks will often cover their eggs when they leave their nest to feed, so perhaps there was doubt in the mind of the pheasant that the nest was already occupied. Why might either of the birds have wanted to share her maternity arrangements with the other? Why was the other agreeable to the arrangement too? If the fox hadn't destroyed the nest we might have been nearer some answers.

Hyperactivity

Spring is in full tilt and there's just such a lot of activity. Most of the songbirds have nestlings, and I watch the parent birds criss-crossing the garden with beaks stuffed with insects. Song thrushes, and the handsomer mistle thrushes, parade across the grass pulling out worms. One lucky young blackbird, newly out of the nest and just able to flutter, was saved by the vigilance of a visiting friend who saw Macbeth preparing to pounce on it. Colin's shout was enough to slow Macbeth down and attract my attention. We all got a rare scolding from the mother bird.

Under-age Smoking

Pruning the elderberry bushes in the garden took me back to caravanning holidays near Ullapool in the 1950s. It was there that I was introduced to illicit childhood smoking by a gamekeeper's son.

He showed me how to remove the dry, spongy pith from inside dead elderberry twigs. To draw the smoke we made a hole in the pith with a needle, and then lit up. I recall that the taste was pretty foul. My clothes and hair must have smelt like an old, reekie lum, and no doubt my parents hoped I'd be violently sick and get the whole thing out of my system quickly.

My chum also recommended smoking tea leaves. At that time you could buy miniature pipes from Woolworths, and as soon as we got home from holiday I invested in one. In the early 1950s my mother only bought loose tea leaves (had tea bags been invented then?) from Coopers or Liptons, so I stuffed the pipe with best Darjeeling. The lady who 'did' for my mother found out (probably the smell gave me away again) and voiced dire warnings about the probability of contracting jaundice. 'The jaundies' she called it, and swore that my skin would turn yellow. Looking back, the experiences didn't come up to expectations, but at the age of seven or eight I really felt a 'bit of a dog' about the whole thing.

Inka is living up to his breed and growing into quite a water dog. We sometimes walk down the side of the Cruick Water and if I throw stones into the water he dives in after them and ducks his head right under in his efforts to retrieve them. Macbeth, with the wisdom of age, looks on admiringly but sees no merit in having two wet dogs drying out in front of the fire.

Family Visit

We Scots don't have a monopoly on thrift. The Doyenne and I are back from a holiday in Brighton in West Sussex where the traditional building style uses Sussex flint. Although some of it was mined – from mines going back to Roman times – most flints were gathered up from fields after ploughing; effectively a free by-product of agriculture.

Old churches and walls, and many of the older houses are built with them. Bound together with chalk and brick they provide a long-lasting weather-resistant outer harling, with a lifetime akin to Aberdeen granite if the age of some of the buildings is anything to go by. Glinting in the sun after rain, the flints are known locally as Sussex 'diamonds'.

It was a family visit to help my sister celebrate a

milestone birthday and she had arranged daily trips into the Sussex countryside. The Sussex Downs are a beautiful part of the south coast, still heavily wooded and predominantly agricultural, with a rich legacy of cultural connections demonstrating the important role the countryside has played in shaping our artistic heritage.

The Downs were a source of inspiration to writers such as Jane Austen, and the poet Tennyson. J. M. W. Turner painted some of his most notable landscapes on the Petworth House Estate. Not far from internationally famous Glyndebourne Opera House is Brinkwells, home of Edward Elgar, where he composed his stunning Cello Concerto in E Minor.

Goodwood Racecourse plays host to the sport of kings and, still on the royal ticket, we visited the splendidly exotic Brighton Royal Pavilion which was built for the Prince Regent who became George IV. The cost of building this extraordinary 'weekend hideaway' was quite staggering. And the cost of preserving and maintaining it today seems no less exorbitant.

But for me the most significant connection with the Downs is the great Reverend Gilbert White of Selborne, who spent a lifetime there ministering to his flock, and whose systematically-recorded observations of the wildlife of his parish single him out as our first true natural historian.

Sadly, we can't really compete with the atmospheric English country pubs. I supped several tasty locally-brewed beers, and there were interesting local cheeses to try, too. I forgot to take a note of their names, but the pleasure's in the memory now.

We were away just five days and returned to fresh green shoots of spring in fields that had been brown earth when we left. We also welcomed our first swallow, although a St Cyrus reader reports she saw a whole summer's-full on Easter Sunday.

And the dogs? They were living it up in spanking new kennels with underfloor heating. Old Sheba will be spinning in her grave at the thought of such decadence! We were all delighted to see each other again and I was near licked half to death.

Living History

Balnamoon, The Rebel Laird was a suitable introduction to my trip up Glen Clova last Sunday to watch the re-enactment of the laying up in 1746, of Ogilvy's, or the Forfarshire Regiment's standard, in Clova Kirk at the head of the glen. The regiment was raised and commanded by Lord David Ogilvy, a direct ancestor of the present Lord Airlie.

The re-enactment was organised by the heritage group Crann Tara, which takes its name from the 'fiery cross', the traditional summoning of the clans to forgather armed for war.

After the Battle of Culloden, at which the Forfarshire Regiment fought for Bonny Prince Charlie, the Angus men marched back to Glen Clova where they were disbanded and their standard laid up for safe-keeping in the small kirk. Kilted in belted plaids (*breacan feile*), and with banners flying, Crann Tara troopers marched down from Loch Brandy which overlooks the glen, on the final leg of the journey taken by their predecessors.

After a service of dedication led by Rev. Malcolm Rooney, Minister of the Glens, the replica regimental standard was accepted by Lord Airlie to be laid up in the kirk, where it is on public view.

The 'Rebel Laird' was James Carnegy of Balnamoon ('Bonnymoon', locally), the house and estate of which name lie west of Brechin, and James was a Captain in the Forfarshire Regiment. After Culloden, many who fought on the Jacobite side fled to the Continent, but James took his chances and slipped across the hills to neighbouring Glen Esk where he took refuge in Balnamoon's Cave which is actually in Glen Mark, a tributary glen of Esk, and is shown on Ordnance Survey maps.

Balnamoon, The Rebel Laird is a novel based on the facts, written by Montrosian John Angus, and recently published by his son Niall. Montrosians of a certain age will remember John's sister, Biddy, who was an art teacher at Montrose Academy.

The story traces Bonnymoon's fugitive months in and around Glen Esk, sheltered from government troops by sympathetic glen folk. Eventually captured and taken to London for trial, his political transgressions were happily dismissed by skilful legal argument. I've walked to lonely Bonnymoon's Cave several times. In reality it could only have been a 'bolt-hole' in times of extreme danger because it is quite one of the most uncomfortable places of refuge you can imagine.

Crann Tara gave a presentation on the arms carried by Ogilvy's soldiers. Before firing a replica Brown Bess flintlock musket those with dogs were advised to take them out of immediate earshot. I'm not surprised – the detonation from just one was formidable. When the whole regiment of 500 discharged their muskets at once the ground must have near shook!

A Sack of Shakings

'Yesterday is history; tomorrow is a mystery; today is a gift. That's why they call it the present.' I've no idea who said it, but what a super thought. The Doyenne and I frequently count our blessings – grandchildren and good health are a start – and we welcome each new morning and the gifts that each day brings.

Small things can leave lasting impressions and whenever I go along familiar paths I'm usually on the lookout for something I've seen before. So I was delighted to see the dipper again – or maybe it was a new one – flying out from beneath a bridge that the dogs and I walk over regularly. I'm wondering if there might be a nest there.

As we continued down the burn two pied wagtails flew on ahead of us, flitting from stone to stone until they'd gone far enough and flew back to where we'd first met them. I looked back and watched them flicking their long tails in disapproval at being disturbed. Little Tommy Wagtails my mother called them when my sister and I were young.

Time spent indoors looking out is mostly time well spent. When you're surrounded by trees and hedges and bushes there's a busy world to look at. A mistle thrush and a jackdaw were squaring up to each other on the grass outside the sitting room window. The thrush was in a right royal rage and attacking the bigger bird. They were well away from cover that might contain a nest so perhaps they were fighting over food. Whatever the reason the thrush won the contest and saw its adversary off.

There's a notice beside the path through the Blue Door at The Burn, near Edzell, which tells you to look out for the otters which live along the River North Esk. I haven't actually seen one there yet, but I've just come in from exploring the riverbank where I found tracks in a wee spit of sand down by the water's edge. They are wary animals and it's either sheer good luck if you see one, or you need perseverance and patience.

The fine weather is welcome but the rivers are low and the spring run of salmon need to get up the rivers to spawn in the headwaters. I've spoken to several fishermen who report little activity. Although the salmon fishing season opened in February for the North and South Esks, anglers should use barbless hooks until 1 June and return all salmon caught on what is called the 'catch and release basis'. This means returning to the river all salmon caught, to help preserve the spring run of fish in the river system.

It's just a sack of shakings this week, but at this time of year there's so much activity it's hard to know what to write about and what to leave out.

Yellow Spring

'Ye canna kiss the lassies when the whin is nae in flooer.' Fortunately, the yellow whin or gorse flowers appear practically all year round, which is lucky for the laddies! Whin and gorse are two names for the same sharp-spined bush which in earlier times was used as fodder for cattle, being bruised to a nutritious pulp by whin mills, examples of which can be seen in agricultural museums. It should make a grand burglar deterrent as it grows quickly into a dense, prickly screen and is painfully uncomfortable to walk through. Not to be outdone, gorse has its own little catchphrase – 'Kissin's not in season when the gorse is not in bloom', which is just the same thing said differently.

Tail Tales

Macbeth has had his spring clip and as usual he arrived home looking like a picture postcard. For twenty-four hours, if we're lucky, he smells fragrant but, sadly, he sees these improving events as an affront to his masculinity and within a day or two he has explored all the darkest, foulest corners and reverted to his more familiar hideous self.

As I was taking the dogs into the vet hospital for their annual vaccinations a boxer puppy sporting a long wavy tail was coming out. The Animal Health and Welfare (Scotland) Act 2006 banned all docking (i.e. the cutting short of an animal's tail) of puppies' tails other than for therapeutic reasons, because the majority of opinion in the Scottish Parliament regarded the practice as mutilation.

I grew up never questioning the wagging stumps of tails on boxers, spaniels, terriers and other breeds which were commonly docked. The undocked tail is, of course, the natural tail but for someone of my age the legislation has resulted in some unusual sights which I am still getting used to. I mentioned this to the vet, who made an interesting comment in relation to show bench breeding and show bench dogs (i.e. dogs exhibited at dog show competitions like Crufts).

For generations these dogs were bred with the precise intention of docking their tails shortly after birth, and their appearance in the show ring reflected the preferences of the judges. As a result of the legislation show judges must now create a new set of standards to define what is the perfect tail. Years of breeding one type of rear-end must now be replaced with years more to find the new millennium, authoritative 'rear of the year'.

Medical Fodder

A tattie, a neep and an ingin
An ingin, a tattie, a neep
An aipple a day keeps the doctor at bay
But an ingin'll dae for a week.

I remember this children's rhyme from my childhood and at the back of my mind is the thought that one of the worthies of the Scottish music halls used to sing it; but, for the life of me, now I couldn't remember who. Mr Bill Mitchell of Monikie wrote to me and solved the problem. The singer was the late Harry Gordon, who was one of the North-East's greatest music hall stars. I've remembered the little ditty for a very long time because Harry Gordon died in 1957.

In the sixteenth and seventeenth centuries 'simples' were medical remedies. So perhaps the humble onion was a universal panacea and the 'simple' way to avoid visiting the medieval horse-doctor's surgery.

When I was a student I developed a ganglion, which

is an uncomfortable fibrous growth on the top of the wrist. The doctor's surgery was a room in his house and when he had examined me he popped out of the room for a moment. He returned with an old, heavy, leather-bound family Bible. He laid my wrist palm down on his desk and struck the ganglion a savage blow with the Bible. 'I've always wanted to try that,' he told me.

Several hundred years ago in rural Scotland, this was an accepted way of dealing with ganglions. Put your trust in the Good Book and all would be well. If the ganglion disintegrated, your faith in the Good Book was well founded and you didn't have to pay the doctor's

bill. If it failed to work you were probably beyond medical and spiritual deliverance, and not even the doctor's intervention could hope to save your loathsome soul.

Looking back it seems obvious that, as a student, I was perceived as little more than medical fodder on whom the doctor could try out his arcane experiments. He asked me to return in a week if the ganglion persisted, but I'd had enough of being a guinea pig, and anyway his treatment actually worked!

I remember one of our granddaughters visiting us and coming into the house in tears of wrathful indignation. She had wandered into a bed of nettles which I had let grow wild in the hope of encouraging butterflies. With homespun enthusiasm I cantered into the garden for a couple of docken leaves, which was my mother's childhood remedy for nettle stings for my sister and me.

My efforts at complementary therapy were not wholly successful. Rubbing the wee hands with the leaves made them green with docken juice but seemingly did little to relieve the discomfort. It's hard to accept that you're a grandfather who can't make nettle stings better, but I'm sure that over the years I've salvaged my shaky reputation.

And, by the way – if you're a committed onion eater who's seeing the doctor twice a week perhaps you're just not believing hard enough in the ingin's restorative powers! And another thing – a more knowledgeable reader than me e-mailed to say that it's the white, sticky juice that you find at the foot of the docken plant when you pull out the leaves that you rub on nettle stings. And here's me thinking for a lifetime that it was the leaves that had 'medicinal compounds'.

Rural Retreats

Birds nest in the most unlikely and, sometimes, apparently impractical places. A pair of blue tits has built their nest a full hand's length inside a rolled-up piece of carpet stored in the barn. Another pair (robins I think, but I didn't come across the nest until the chicks had fledged) had to complete a major construction inside a box of books before the hen could start laying. There was a space four or five inches deep between the books which they had to fill with dead beech leaves, grass and moss, before they could get on with the nest proper. It seemed unnecessarily hard work when there were so many other holes and ledges in the building which would have been just as suitable.

It brought to mind the paella dish which I took down from a high shelf in the garden shed to find that it too had been converted into a nest. The dish was forty-two centimetres across, or sixteen inches if you're my generation, and the birds had to complete exceptional foundation works with moss and beech leaves and dry grasses to stabilise the nest in the centre of the dish.

From the Doyenne's Kitchen

ROAST PORK AND SAVOURY PUDDINGS

When I first came to Scotland I was surprised how little pork featured in the butchers' shops. In Yorkshire there were Pork Butchers who sold only pork and pork products: bacon, ham, sausages, pork pies, brawn and anything else you could make from pork! We ate a lot of pork and when we had a roast we always had savoury puddings with it. They are a huge favourite with the family and grandchildren, and really take a trick at a lunch or supper party with friends.

A roast of pork *must* have the skin on it, and that skin must be scored to make the crackling. Crispy crackling is second only to the savoury puddings!

3 oz breadcrumbs
1 onion, finely chopped
2 oz suet
1 heaped teaspoon self-raising flour
1 egg
I heaped teaspoon rubbed sage
⅓ pint milk to mix
Salt and pepper

Method
Soak the breadcrumbs in the milk for 5 minutes. Add the chopped onion, suet, flour and sage and mix with the egg. Season with salt and freshly ground pepper.

Brush a 12 cup bun tin with a little oil and spoon in the mixture. Cook in a hot oven for approximately 30 minutes until crisp and brown on the top.

MAY

Full of Promise

One of the countryside's busiest months when everything on mountain, moor, coastline, wood, riverbank and loch is fully occupied mating, nesting, breeding and raising their young. Beech, oak and sycamore are all in full leaf and insect life is abundant. Enjoy nature's colourful palette and the rewards of talking to grandchildren.

The Stick Maker

May is a favourite month for walking the dogs, so full of promise and fresh colours heralding the coming summer. Spring wild flowers are everywhere and there's such variety of colour and size and shape. I've picked marsh marigolds, or kingcups as they are sometimes known, down beside the stream and wispy celandine grows along the roadside verge. Patches of blue wild violets have appeared in the wood, as have blue and white wild hyacinths, though they may be garden bulbs which have been thrown out and gone wild. The trees are bursting with the vitality of burgeoning growth. One swallow doesn't make a summer, but as five greeted us last Sunday, lined up on the telephone wire, surely our prospects are hopeful.

Driving from Friockheim to Forfar on the A932, just before the turn-off to rather grand sounding Trumperton, the woods are carpeted with delicate wood anemones with blushing pink petals and fern-like leaves. They flourish in shady places in deciduous woods from March to around the end of May, so I stopped the car and walked back to enjoy them while they are at their best.

Several years ago I cut three straight branches that I thought I could make into sticks. They have dried out quite naturally and I tried my hand at turning them into the finished article. Nothing very fancy you'll understand, just the first efforts of a complete amateur. I trimmed off the side twigs and sanded them down and shaped the tops into a comfortable smooth handle. Only a couple of hours work per stick, but what a lot of simple pleasure it's given me. My father was clever with his hands and a very good carpenter. I've never been able to match his skills but I keep my eyes open for more suitable sticks, which is an added interest when I'm out with those dogs.

I found Macbeth, front paws on the trunk of a tree, gazing intently up into the branches. We had disturbed one of the local red squirrels which had been foraging amongst the beech mast which lies thick on the ground. Macbeth believes that if he runs very fast he will catch one. This squirrel wasn't going to hang around, and was off up the tree before Macbeth had left the starting blocks. I've explained to him on several occasions that compared to a squirrel his ratio of leg length to body volume means he doesn't stand an earthly. Macbeth rejects simple science and continues to put his faith in pious hope. I cannot share his confidence.

Outdoor Snooker Championship

Yellow, green and brown, the colours of the first three balls on the snooker table, were the predominant colours of the countryside as I drove down to Dunblane. It was the way my mind was working, having stayed up the previous evening to watch Mark Williams beat Ken Doherty to become the 2003 World Snooker Champion.

Representing the yellow ball were great splashes of bright yellow oilseed rape in full bloom. The fresh, young shoots of barley and wheat provided the green ball. Some is sown in autumn and is known as the winter crop. Interspersed were brown fields, newly planted with potatoes that hadn't yet made their appearance. It was a cracking spring morning and the sky was clear blue. As I passed Perth Aerodrome pink and white cherry blossom was frothing on the trees lining the entrance. The postie's red van went rattling up a farm road, maybe to deliver some unwelcome bills, but hopefully a couple of welcome cheques!

And what would provide the black ball to complete my snooker table? I didn't see it till I was on my journey home. In a field across the road from Glamis village stood a pure black Highland bull – or was she a cow? I'd only ever seen the red breed before, but there he was with the distinctive wide sweep of horns. My old friend Angus Davidson, retired from farming at Glen Effock, near the head of Glen Esk, could tell me that while this variety isn't common, they are not so unusual to breeders. It all made me wonder whether snooker could become an outdoor sport! (I'd forgotten when I wrote this article that some years ago the Doyenne and I visited a herd of blonde Highlanders on a farm somewhere near Nethybridge, in Inverness-shire.)

Web of Mystery

Mad May hares are a twist on our ideas of mad March ones. Macbeth and I watched three playing together in the middle of a field of spring barley. They weren't as boisterous as their March counterparts, which rear up on their hind legs, shadow boxing with each other. The March aggression is part of a courtship ritual and happens when unreceptive females, not yet ready to mate, fight off the unwanted overtures of testosterone-fuelled males that are ready to mate. These three were playing their own version of tag and, after the wild, rainy days at the start of the month, were enjoying the fading heat of the late afternoon sun.

After a number of optimistic predictions in these Saturday pieces, I'm beginning to hope that the hares may really be making a quiet comeback after many years of absence. I've never found a definitive explanation for their sudden and almost wholesale drop in numbers in the 1960s, but they are bonny animals and I like to see them in the fields.

I've watched occasional single hares when I've been out with Macbeth, although they are always as wary as the very devil. The moment they see us they are off over the horizon. One did 'flap' down, flattening itself as low as possible in the growing barley, its long ears laid along its back until it looked just like a large stone out in the field. Hares have a keenly developed sense of self-preservation, and the moment it sensed it was no longer in my line of vision it was away. When I looked back all I saw were the powerful hind legs steadily disappearing over a rise in the ground and the long, radar-like ears flickering to pick up every friendly and hostile message.

The wrens, which took over the swallows' nest under the eaves, have hatched their eggs. I've found two of their tiny empty white shells lying in the gravel. Several times we've watched swallows flying up to the commandeered nest as if expecting to use it themselves, and heard the angry commotion of complaints when they realised it had been hijacked by squatters!

I remember the nest well when its new occupants had finished converting it for their own use. The wrens had reduced its size for their own requirements, lining it with moss and dried grasses. I felt sympathy for the swallows which had flown several thousands of miles from their winter quarters in Africa and got dog's abuse (in a wren manner of speaking) when they tried to re-occupy their old home. They soon gave up the unequal struggle.

After a humid night I took Macbeth for his early morning run – it was just the sort of morning Sheba used to enjoy. She would step outside to taste the day and after several deep exploratory sniffs, and deciding everything was satisfactory, was ready for the day's excitement. The early sun was shining on the beech hedge alongside the road. Spiders had been very busy overnight, for spun in amongst the beech twigs were hundreds, if not thousands, of spiders' webs still covered in beads of dew reflecting in the sunlight. Spiders are not my favourite insect, but I'm intrigued by their abilities to spin such complete works of art whose only purpose is to snare their creators' next meal. It all makes a lot of sense to the spiders, but is a bit chilling for their victims.

Natural Remedies

Out and about with the dogs there is plenty of evidence of spring's progress. I especially enjoy the wee flashes of blue and yellow in the woods and hedgerows. The field behind the kitchen is filled with petite yellow wild pansies, or heartsease. Common violets and speedwell, and the early forget-me-nots have just enough time to announce their presence before they are shouldered aside by sprouting undergrowth.

I did some research into the derivation of the country names for these wild plants, which have such grand Latin descriptions for such, mostly, tiny flowers. Heartsease was used to treat a wide range of afflictions. On the one hand it was a laxative, and on the other it was highly regarded as a love potion, which seems something of a contradiction. However, these little blue wild pansies sound like powerful medicine and if they were as efficacious as they sound, small wonder our ancestors experienced an 'easy heart' as they looked forward to a rapid recovery.

A hapless knight was picking a bouquet of flowers for his lady love by the side of a rushing stream. He slipped and tumbled into the foaming waters. As he was swept to his doom he threw the spray of flowers back to his love with the fateful words, 'forget-me-not.'

Speedwell was also traditionally valued for its medicinal properties. I learnt that it should be 'given in good broth of a hen', and that it was used as a specific against 'pestilential fevers'. It was an accepted cure for bronchial troubles, but I like the idea that it was also widely used to treat 'the itch'.

Medieval itch would have needed more than a good scratch if you wanted to get well speedily!

The Speedwell, of course, was the sister ship of *The Mayflower*, (another traditional physic) which took the Pilgrim Fathers to America in 1620. John Whitson was Lord Mayor of, and Member of Parliament for, Bristol, and one of the city's Merchant Venturers or entrepreneurs. There is a family tradition that he was one-time owner of *The Mayflower*, but that by 1620 he had sold her, and the Pilgrim Fathers chartered her from the new owners.

The story is that *The Mayflower* needed a new set of sails to undertake the long voyage to the New World, and the Pilgrim Fathers sought John Whitson's help. He agreed to supply the sails on condition that the adventurers took Cheviot wool with them to trade for native goods, which would be sent back to England by way of profit.

It's unlikely old John was an ancestor, for another family tradition is that the Scottish Whitsons are all descended from three Viking brothers. But it's a good story, and there are enough grains of credibility about it to think it might be true.

More Natural Remedies

I'm thankful I did some homework before writing last week's piece. There was an almost immediate response on the phone, followed by a most interesting letter. It confirmed what I had already deduced, that for every story about nature's remedies there's another one to cap it.

At the core of homeopathic healing is the belief that there is a herbal remedy for almost every ill suffered by man. And not only mankind; the writer mentions some of the traditional remedies being used to cure racing pigeons.

The workaday aspirin was developed from an extract of willow trees, yet how many of us consider its natural credentials as we anticipate the relief that the pills provide?

It all seems to boil down to a matter of personal belief, but you'd need a pretty robust personal belief for some of the treatments. My correspondent recalled his grandmother's experience of ailing children, who weren't 'making up', being given a spoonful of the clear serum found in a new-laid cow pat. You'd certainly want to hold your nose as you swallowed that one!

Law of Nature

It was Inka racing ahead that startled the meadow pipit out of its nest on the ground directly in front of me. The nest was built inside a small grass tussock, scarcely large enough to conceal it, and inside were four brown mottled eggs. I passed it two days later and stopped for a moment to see if the chicks had hatched, but the nest was empty. Some predator, a crow I suspect, had enjoyed a tasty snack.

All for Love

'Four and twenty blackbirds baked in a pie' – driving through Edzell, our neighbouring village, earlier in the week I nearly clobbered the first two. Two blackies (blackbirds) shot out of a garden on my side of the road, one in hot pursuit of the other. They streaked between me and the car in front and were in danger of meeting an untimely end, splattered across the windscreen of an oncoming car. There was a tremendous exhibition of split-second aerobatics and they scraped their way out of terminal danger.

I'd hardly gone a couple of miles down the road when I saw two more beside the gates of Keithock House, knocking seven bells out of each other and quite oblivious to traffic speeding by scarcely a foot from them. It's not too late for blackbirds to be nesting so perhaps several particularly agreeable hen birds were the cause of all the controversy, and were waiting on the sidelines in a spirit of winner takes all!

It's a time of year when birds and animals can temporarily lose all sense of personal danger as nature's urges spill over and take control. Years ago driving home in the five o'clock rush in Minto Street, one of Edinburgh's busiest roads, all the cars had to take evasive action round two stray dogs, inelegantly united, and to blazes with the indignant hooting and tooting of horns!

Mothtly About Moths

There are about ten times more species of moth than there are of butterflies. I know this now because I've been speaking to a man who has been a lifetime enthusiast about these nocturnal aviators. We met as the evening was turning to dusk and he was setting up his moth trap. This is a round perspex dome, lit throughout the night by a mercury vapour bulb which attracts the insects. The temperature was rather cool which is not good for mothing, so it was unlikely he would equal his best night's catch of 212 moths early in April. The pussy willows were out then and the nectar from the flowers is an important food source for the macro moths, energising the process of mating and laying their eggs.

I learnt about the Common Quaker, the Hebrew Character and the Clouded Drab which have wing-spans of up to an inch. Many species spend winter as a pupa in their adult state, ready to hatch when the right weather conditions trigger activation, and then they have only a short lifespan. Some migrating species, such as the large Death Head hawk moth, float across from the Continent on wind currents. It has an image of a skull and crossbones on the back of its head and if you touch it, it squeaks like a mouse – which all sounds a bit unnerving!

Next morning the moth man was pleased with his catch, which was resting docilely on old egg boxes in the base of the trap. It's obvious when you're told, but, of course, their daytime is our night-time and vice versa, so they were all sound asleep! Because they are so vulnerable during daylight hours they have wonderfully complex camouflage. One of the small micro moths was coloured and veined in light grey, just like a piece of dead lichen on a tree. Another could easily have been mistaken for a shrivelled-up beech leaf. I shan't think of moths as lampshade marauders any longer – they are another fascinating strand of nature that I want to know more about.

Listening to Silence

Fresh ideas from a young mind are entertaining and stimulating, so I was pleased when grandson James joined me to walk the dogs. We took the track through the woods to the small loch which lies about three quarters of a mile behind the house. I wanted to see if the pair of cormorants I had written about some weeks back were still there. There was no sign of the birds, so we leant our elbows on the gate and had a good 'hing' (a very Scottish activity originating from people hanging out of their windows to watch the world pass by), while we contemplated the view. There's a rickle of dead branches not far off and there must be some very beckoning scents beneath it, because the dogs make a beeline for it each time we walk there.

It was fine standing in companionable silence – grandson and grandfather didn't need to talk all the time to know we were enjoying the moment. It's a happy landscape we live in with so much to see and hear, and quiet reflection is one of the best ways to take it all in. Soon enough the noise of Macbeth's efforts to get deeper in beneath the branches, and Inka's efforts to follow him, broke the spell and after imprecations and threats of what would happen if they didn't get back to heel immediately, we headed for home along the side of the burn.

Several years ago, I taught James to make a whistle with a blade of grass stretched between his thumbs. He decided it was time to whistle up the wind again and the peace was shattered with the shrill screech of vibrating grass. It obviously struck a chord with the cattle on the far side of the field which galloped across to investigate the strange sound. Perhaps there's a fortune there for James if he can patent a grass whistle to 'call the cattle home.'

We spoke about his ideas for the future and he thought an outdoors life was more to his liking than a desk-bound job. I've done a bit of both and I can understand his preference. We watched swallows swooping and diving just inches from the ground, feeding hard on airborne insects to see them through the night. Most of their lives are spent on the wing and it's staggering to think there's so much energy stored in such a small frame, and that it's fuelled only by flying beasties.

As we got back into the wood we heard the most awful commotion coming from above our heads. At first I thought it must be small songbirds mobbing a jackdaw or a jay which was threatening eggs or chicks. We investigated and found that the noise came from a hole about twelve feet up the trunk of a beech tree. It was a nest of very vocal nestlings hungrily waiting on their parent birds to return with the next course for tea. I went back later and watched jackdaws flying in and out, so there was our answer.

Choir Practice

Eight minutes past four o'clock in the morning was an unholy hour to be wakened. It was the milkman delivering milk to the 'big hoose.' I watched the van lights swing round the walls of the bedroom as he headed off to rouse the next unsuspecting soul who thought he had at least another three hours peaceful slumber.

It seemed I wasn't the only one to be jolted awake by the disturbance. The first glimmers of daytime were lightening up the sky and, first, just a single birdsong greeted the hesitant dawning. The repetition of each phrase identified it as a song thrush. I'd already found one of its spotted sky-blue eggs lying empty at the side of the drive, dropped far from the nest to draw attention away from its chicks. Next a chaffinch piped up and in no time the 'hale unseemly crew' had chimed in and the dawn chorus was echoing from every treetop. I wasn't going to get to sleep again so I toddled down to the kitchen to make a cup of tea.

At the end of March I wrote about the mistle thrush that had nested in a particularly exposed position in the fork of a tree. They normally lay four eggs but I could only see two chicks that she raised. They are fledged now and have left the nest but aren't fully independent yet and rely on the parent birds for supplementary feeding. We see the parent birds working tirelessly over the lawn at the front of the house, hunting for worms and creepy crawlies which are the thrushes' delight.

Everything and everyone in the countryside is busy right now. Fields are full of tattie-planting machines as the farmers get the last of their harvest into the ground. One farmer I spoke to commented that after all the splendid dry weather it was really time we had some rain! As a wee laddie I went out to Stone of Morphie Farm between Montrose and St Cyrus and, sitting in a horse-drawn cart, watched the potatoes being planted by hand. The seed potatoes were held in a jute sack tied round the waist and at every step the farm worker dropped a potato into the furrow, and they were then 'furred up', or covered over with earth in the traditional ridges.

When the crop was lifted, again by hand, the potatoes were stored in a straw-lined pit called a 'tattie clamp'. To protect them from the winter frosts they were covered with more straw and topped over with several inches of earth.

Although they are mainly nocturnal animals I found a hedgehog snuffling around in the afternoon sunshine. It paid no attention to me and I was able to get to within about a yard from it without disturbing it. It was a different story when it became aware of Macbeth and it curled up instantly in its distinctive protective ball.

Seen from Afar

A birthday present of binoculars has opened up a new world for me. The family all chipped in to buy them and now I hardly leave the house to walk the dogs without my new toy around my neck. The amount of activity amongst the birdlife, in particular, make it one of the best times of year to enjoy the benefits of extended vision. Migrant visitors like the willow warblers and the swallows have arrived and, along with all the native birds, are preoccupied with nesting and breeding. For the time being they are less wary about us humans and provide endless entertainment from the kitchen window. But it's up at the lochan at the back of the house that I'm having most fun.

There are now five families of mallard which have hatched and I can watch the ducklings clearly from a distance, scampering amongst the reeds fringing the shore. As soon as the mother birds are aware of the dogs they call their broods off onto the safety of the water. A wigeon drake patrols up and down a stretch at the top of the loch. He's a handsome devil with chestnut-coloured feathers on his head, broken by a creamy-buff forehead and crown. His mate will be tucked away on her well-camouflaged nest of eggs not too far from the waterside.

The tufted duck has laid her eggs too, as has the coot whose white wattle flash I see peeping above the untidy nest which it has built on a semi-submerged branch some yards out from the shore. A family of dab-chicks (little grebes) will be hatching soon. Curlews, tumbling peewits with their wistful, plaintive calls, and oyster catchers call in for a wash and a brush-up in the shallows at the top of the loch.

A speculative heron glided in hoping, perhaps, for a snack of young frogs or an eel. Like a tall grey senti-nel, with eyes apparently half-closed, it hardly seemed interested in the world around it. Scarcely disturbing the water it cautiously waded through the shallows, but the merest ripple below the surface will galvanise it into action and the pick-axe bill strikes at its prey with lightning efficiency. Endlessly patient, they are one of the bird world's most efficient killers.

And there's so much else to hear and see. Dozy bumble bees, and wasps that come into the house and have to be dealt with. I've seen just one butterfly, a peacock, and rather hoped that if I'd seen one I'd see some more – but not so far. Perhaps it's still a bit early. Thinking back, the hedgerows and the woodland fringes used to be so busy with a host of the pretty insects. I paid little attention to them then and just took them for granted. They were so common and now it's quite a treat to see one.

Less welcome are the ticks which both dogs have been picking up – or more correctly the ticks which attach themselves to the dogs. Ticks are parasitical feeders, i.e. they live by feeding on the blood of host animals like the dogs. They look, and are, pretty disgusting insects and can be a cause of illness in your animals. They are mostly found in woodland areas where there is heavy undergrowth, which of course is where we regularly walk. So at this time of year when they are at their most active I regularly check the dogs to see if they have acquired any of these unwelcome callers.

Traditionally, margarine rubbed on, or a drop of paraffin painted on suffocates them and they eventually fall off. But son-in-law Gibson bought me a special tick remover which nicks them off cleanly and I then put a dab of Germolene on the spot to disinfect it.

From the Doyenne's Kitchen

RACK OF LAMB WITH MINT SAUCE

We keep several pots outside the kitchen door filled with herbs. The most prolific is sage and I pick bunches and dry them in the winter to put in the savoury puddings. Parsley, mint, thyme and new shoots on the rosemary bush are all marshalled into the spring menus.

Angus just loves lamb and as a special treat I'll cook a rack of lamb, French trimmed by the butcher, so you have the succulent 'eyes' of lamb and all the fat trimmed off. I make slits in the lamb and push in sprigs of rosemary and slivers of garlic. Spread on a little dripping and cook in a hot oven for about 35 minutes so it's still nice and pink in the middle.

Served with fresh mint sauce and homemade red-currant jelly, what could be better? Young broad beans should be available now, and served in a parsley sauce they are a delicious accompaniment to the lamb along with some new potatoes.

FRESH MINT SAUCE

A large handful of mint leaves
1 tablespoon caster sugar
2 tablespoons boiling water
3 tablespoons white wine vinegar
Pinch of salt

Method

Wash and dry the mint leaves and spread on a board. Sprinkle the leaves with the caster sugar and chop them finely (the sugar makes it easier to chop them). Put in a small bowl and add the boiling water. This will 'set' the colour of the mint. Allow to cool slightly then stir in the vinegar and salt. Taste and add more vinegar or sugar if necessary.

JUNE

Unlikely Stories

Butterflies plundering garden flowers for nectar. Warmer evenings mean more moth activity. Foxgloves in forgotten woody corners, dog roses by the roadsides, bramble and honeysuckle flowering in the hedgerow. Nature red in tooth and claw, young life and the folly of dog owners! And a story you won't believe.

Birds of a Feather

I've just finished reading a thoroughly entertaining book called *How to be a Bad Birdwatcher* by Simon Barnes, which is both witty and informative. I can empathise with the author completely, for he started birdwatching with little more than enthusiasm. I like his description of his hobby: 'the calm delight of the utterly normal, and the rare and sudden delight of the utterly unexpected.'

Calming the Soul

I've been out with my strimmer, battling with nettles which are the most invasive of weeds. I've purposely left a patch in an out-of-the-way corner of the garden in the hope that butterflies will lay their eggs on the leaves, the resultant caterpillars will then feed on them and, in the course of time, transform into more butterflies, adding more pleasure to the garden. Butterflies used to be such a common sight – Red admirals, tortoiseshells, peacocks, cabbage whites and others that I saw and took for granted and whose names I never knew, all were widespread when I was young. Now it's something notable to see even one, and their loss to our gardens is a bit of a disaster. The Doyenne and I have five grandchildren and I wonder what sort of countryside our great-grandchildren will grow up in.

The leaves on the trees are all now fully opened and walks with the dogs in the woods generate a different mood. The wonderful canopy of green above us creates a feeling of quiet seclusion. In winter, the bare trees provide some protection from the wind, but at this time of year the fluttering barrier of leaves calms even the wildest wind, dissipating it and scattering its force.

Friends from the south visited recently and walked in the local woods. They saw buzzards, pheasants, a red squirrel and two roe deer. It was all special but the red squirrel was a real treat for them as grey squirrels have taken over the woodlands where they normally walk. It does me good to be reminded how lucky we are round here to be still surrounded by wildlife that was commonplace everywhere fifty years ago.

Random Thoughts

How many drivers leaving Brechin noticed the oystercatcher sitting on her nest in the middle of the roundabout at the access slip road to the dual carriageway? It says something about the bird's instinctive trust that passing vehicles won't pose a danger, that she felt secure enough to nest there. It's just a scraping in the dust and pebbles, and the sitting bird was very conspicuous, but the constant traffic probably protected her from the attentions of hunting raptors. I saw that at least one chick had been successfully hatched (they lay two, sometimes three, eggs), so it's been a bit of a success story.

By contrast, Arthur Grewar had a sad story to tell. Making a final evening round of his lambs he came across a dead otter by the side of the dual carriageway. It was still bleeding so had only recently been killed. The fading light at dusk, too much speed, too little attention, possibly ignorance of wildlife – all may have contributed. Otters aren't exactly an endangered species but there aren't enough of them around for even one to be wantonly run down.

'Cow parsley' is a bit of a botanical misnomer in my view. It doesn't look the least like parsley and the expert opinions I have canvassed doubt whether cows eat it. On the other hand, horses apparently love it. Such a common plant, its white, lacy flowers atop tall green stems appear in neglected corners of gardens, roadsides and the edges of fields.

I was bowling round a corner on the way to Brechin and just had time to notice what I thought was a buzzard on the grass verge. I braked and indeed it was. Very slowly I reversed and saw that it was 'mantling' something which it must have just brought down. Holding their prey in their talons they stand over it with their wings outstretched, like a cape or mantle, to prevent it escaping. It flew off before I could see what the prey was but the dusty blue pigeon feather lying in the grass may have been a clue.

A thoughtful friend lent me *A Country Life* by Sir Roy Strong; art historian, museum curator, writer, broadcaster, landscape designer and one-time youngest Director of the Victoria and Albert Museum. It is a compilation of a monthly diary he contributed to *Country Life* magazine. For a relative newcomer like myself it is especially interesting to compare my own style with that of a more established writer. It's a delightful book that's worth a read.

Spitting's Rude

'Cuckoo spit' appears everywhere on the tall grasses in our favourite walking wood. It's another name-eccentricity from past generations and has nothing to do with cuckoos or spit. It certainly looks like spit – a bubbly, white blob sticking to the grass leaves. The Doyenne, who is an authority on many matters, thinks it is a deposit left by an insect. After some research I have discovered that the frothy, white 'spittle' conceals a sap-sucking insect called a froghopper, and the spit is a protection against hungry predators.

Two glittering eyes transfixed me. At the foot of the hedge a young thrush crouched motionless. It had grown too large for the nest but still relied on the parent birds for food. It still had its juvenile beak, as wide as it was long, ever ready to open and receive the endless supply of bugs and beasties so patiently brought by the parents. The moment I took my eye off it its natural sense of survival took over and it whisked out of sight into the cover of the undergrowth.

By a busy roadside a young peewit, all long legs waiting for its body to grow into them, was confused by the constant traffic. It didn't know whether to try and cross the road or jump back into the undergrowth again. They are very fragile looking at this stage and look constantly surprised – which of course they may very well be!

Driving from Brechin to Forfar and passing the gates of Careston Castle I saw a black rabbit in the field opposite. They were called 'parsons' when I was a youngster, but it has been years since I heard anyone refer to them so.

The longest day, the summer solstice, occurred last Saturday, 21 June. I suppose we should have all gone out at daybreak and washed our faces in the morning dew, or danced around a blazing fire in the gloaming. It was far more fun to be invited out to supper, talk with congenial friends, enjoy good food and wine, and watch the evening fade into the not-quite darkness that characterises the night hours at this time of year.

Macbeth has had his hair clipped. 'A country gentleman's summer haircut' was what I asked Debbie for. He went in looking like a badly rolled-up ball of string and emerged looking like he'd just stepped off a whisky label. But Macbeth is always up for that sort of challenge. It was barely twenty-four hours and he was back to his normal mobile midden state.

The Hunted and the Hunter

Spring turning to summer displays itself in many ways. The hawthorn trees are in full bloom and their blossom this year seems as abundant and profuse as ever I can remember. Driving round the country roads I've seen cascades of the creamy ivory flowers smothering the branches and weighing them down.

A hen pheasant clattered across the farm steading hoping to divert my attention from her clutch of chicks scampering for the safety of a hedge. They were only recently hatched with browny stripes on their heads and upper body – just fluffy bundles of feathers on skinny wee legs.

All but one reached safety and the last one froze amongst the stones hoping its camouflage would hide it from my sight. I stood quite still and watched. Wee cheeps were coming from the hedge bottom as the other chicks kept in contact with their mother.

My man started to lose his nerve and began cheeping too so as not to become isolated from the rest of his family. Suddenly he could stand it no longer and raced towards the cover, scrambling over chuckie stones that to him were probably the size of boulders.

I watched a buzzard being mobbed by rooks. It kept coming back and being chased away each time. I imagine there were young rooks close by and the parents saw no good reason why their offspring should be served up as supper to young buzzards.

Another buzzard, looking about the size of a starling, was circling miles high above the house. A tiny, single-seater, microlight aeroplane, open to the elements, with just a flimsy fabric wing and what sounded like a motor-mower engine, went sailing past at much the same height. I wonder who was more surprised – the pilot or the buzzard?

Nature's Bounty

A year ago I wrote about 'lucy arnots', which are the edible tubers of pig or ground nuts. I promised myself that this year I'd look for some. Arthur Grewar, who knows where to find any of nature's free food, took me to the banks of the River South Esk where the plants grow in profusion. It involved more digging than I expected, but was worth the effort.

The knobbly 'nuts' look like root ginger and lie up to four inches below the surface. I soaked them and scraped the skin off, and tried my first one. They taste like hazelnuts initially, but there is a spicy aftertaste reminiscent of radish, so we sliced some up to add a bit of zing to the barbecue salad.

From The Doyenne's Kitchen

JUNGLE JUICE

This recipe for a countryside cordial is a family favourite for barbecues and long, lazy evenings at weekends.

It is inexpensive and very summery, but be warned it is more alcoholic than you might think.

Method

Mix a bottle of cheap white wine with an equal amount of lemonade. Add four tablespoons of Cointreau, plenty of ice and slices of cucumber and orange. Bruise a handful of mint leaves (spearmint if possible) between your palms to release the flavour, and stir in.

Once the juice is finished the boozy cucumber and orange slices are delicious eaten with ice cream. I don't approve of my husband's name for the recipe, 'Virgin's milk.'

SUMMER SALAD DRESSING

All our family and their spouses are imaginative cooks. Our son-in-law Gibson has provided this quickly prepared summer salad dressing for barbecues. Because the ingredients are measured by volume you can make only as much as you need at any one time.

1 part balsamic vinegar
2 parts freshly squeezed orange juice
2 parts olive oil
Grind of black pepper

Mix together in a bowl.

Warm Welcome

The woodpeckers have been the stars of the garden show this week. A family comes to the bird table each morning and they provide endless diversion. The Doyenne called me to watch two 'peckers feeding together on a peanut feeder. It didn't last long, however, because the smaller female attacked the bigger male and chased him off. He couldn't hang onto the wire mesh any longer when she began to peck his bottom. I sympathised with his dilemma but when he flew onto the bird table and the female began to feed him, it was clear he was still a young bird.

Macbeth's shrill barking had me at the front door to see what was happening. Inka was capering round a rolled-up hedgehog, trying to work out how to pick it up – to present to the Doyenne as a wee gift, no doubt. Macbeth, as senior dog, took the initiative and lifted his leg on it. Not discouraged by such a warm welcome the hedgehog was back in the garden a couple of days later. Inka got just as excited, and Macbeth? – I hardly need tell you!

Squirrelling Away

'If you want a story, here's one you won't believe.' Well, there was a red rag to a bull and I just had to hear it. This is the fifth year of writing my column and I've learnt not to dismiss any stories about nature and wild-life, however unlikely they may seem at first.

An angler was fishing on the River North Esk some way below Edzell. He noticed a red squirrel running along the riverbank towards him. To steady himself he put his hand on a boulder by the riverbank and the

squirrel, apparently quite fearless and scarcely breaking step, jumped onto the boulder, ran up his arm and
perched on his hat.

After a few moments there seemed nothing of interest to delay it further, so the squirrel ran down his
arm and went on its way. They are such timid animals
normally that he could only think it was a youngster
that hadn't learnt how perilous a young squirrel's life
can be. His story reminded me of a photograph I saw
in a book about the Earl Grey of the time, with a tame
robin which would perch on his hat whenever he went
into his garden.

My fisherman had another squirrel tale to tell. He
watched an adult squirrel, which seemed to have an
odd growth round its neck that restricted its movement, hopping its way across a piece of rough ground
and over his garden dyke. It wasn't until it was in the
garden that he realised that it was hampered by one of
its young that was clinging to its chest and neck.

Mother and kit got tree-borne and my fisherman
followed them as they swung through the branches
to the far side of the garden where the mother deposited the youngster in an owl nesting box that had
been put up to encourage tawny owls. She went back
for two more kits, so she must have been delighted to
have found such a convenient ready-made drey for
her family. And the owls just had to wait until vacant
possession could be resumed.

In the same vein, out with the dogs I was excited
to see something I hadn't seen for maybe forty years.

We disturbed a bird which flew clumsily out of old rhododendrons into a wee stand of birch trees. It was a woodcock airlifting one of its young to safety, clutched between its thighs and claws. Normally, when alarmed, these birds jink and jouk at high speed to confuse pursuers but, like the mother squirrel, this woodcock's mobility was hampered.

Inka was very interested in what was under the spreading canopy of a large tree – interestingly a split-leaf beech tree which produces two different types of leaf. I got him away and went to investigate. It was a pheasant's nest with eighteen eggs in it. That's worse than the old lady who lived in a shoe!

An Irish Blue Moon

An Irishman told us – the Doyenne and me, that is – where the expression 'once in a blue moon' came from. It's when a second full moon occurs in a single calendar month. The moon isn't actually blue, of course, and why it should be so described the Irishman did not say. The explanation was unimportant for we were on the west coast of Ireland, staying in a holiday cottage in Connemara, about six miles from the hotel where we spent our honeymoon in 1965.

The Irishman explained further that the weather at the time of a blue moon is a forecast of the weather for the ensuing month. There had been just such a moon at the end of May and the weather had been fine and sunny. The rain had tipped down from the moment we got off the car ferry at Belfast and continued every mile of the way to our destination at Ballynakill Bay. By next morning the skies had cleared and we had ten days of constant sunshine – practically unheard of in that part of Ireland – but it confirmed the Irishman's weather-forecasting skills.

Away from the tyranny of the telephone, and surrounded by quite magnificent scenery, we set out to revive past happy times. The Twelve Pins Mountains preside over a countryside which is surprisingly reminiscent of Sutherland in North-west Scotland. You're never far from water – sea or loughs (note Irish spelling) and rivers are round most corners.

Connemara has transformed itself from the place we remembered. The natural feature of thatched cottages has been lost from the Connemara landscape because today's homebuyers want contemporary homes with modern amenities. In place of the cottages are new and substantial houses, more often than not two stories, and what seems to be an indicator of essential style – a grand set of gates at the end of each drive.

It's unrealistic to expect people to maintain a lifestyle that would be hopelessly outdated. The traditional Irish thatched cottage was one of the most evocative and appealing sights for visitors but it's a sight that appears now to have gone forever.

What we were unprepared for was the diversity of

wildlife. There aren't great numbers of any one species, but in this wildlife paradise nature coexists very comfortably with man and we had some exciting sightings. Great northern divers which I've only ever seen once before, and a pair of ravens. Most unexpected of all was my first sighting of a pair of choughs – I didn't know they bred on the west coast of Ireland. Cuckoos greeted us in the morning and were the last sound we heard at night. And the Doyenne watched an otter ambling across the road.

It's clear we go to Connemara but once in a blue moon, but after this holiday I think I'd like to return rather sooner.

Party Animals

There's an enthusiasm for their dogs' welfare that grips some dog owners and which non-dog owners might regard as so misplaced as to border on lunacy. And it troubles me to admit that the Doyenne and I appear to be slipping into the 'barking' category.

We all received an invitation – dogs, Doyenne and me, that is – to a 'surprise' first birthday party on Montrose beach for Kiwi, a black Labrador. Races and fun were promised but 'hopefully no fights,' which rather took the edge off the event for Macbeth. One lead per dog was recommended – even at his most ferocious, one lead is enough for Macbeth.

Our hosts undertook to provide fresh water for dogs (I've seen dogs trying to drink seawater and they really don't enjoy it). A birthday cake was promised and any dog-loving human would have been proud to be the recipient of the handsome confection. It seemed a bit hard that it wasn't shared with the dogs whose day it was meant to be.

There were races on the beach for dogs – with prizes. I'm afraid with his little sawn-off legs Macbeth stood no chance. If Inka had had his wits about him I'm quite sure he was speedy enough to have won his category. For reasons best known to himself he ran in the opposite direction so we went home empty-handed.

I had been a prophet of doom beforehand, predicting that dogs would run off and we'd be picking them up at Stonehaven before the day was out. Our two had been in kennels for a fortnight while we were on holiday in Ireland and they gloried in being able to run free. Dogs can display their emotions very clearly and it was a pleasure to see them so obviously enjoying themselves. If there was a problem, it was that there were so many black Labs it was difficult to identify 'our boy' in the mêlée.

Nothing was overlooked in the preparations for the day – there was even a spade to dispose of unwelcome 'memories'. The only mad ones were the humans who went out in pouring rain – against which we have no natural protection – wearing wellies, waxed jackets, bunnets and some even sporting umbrellas.

As the party ended the wind was blowing a fine spray off the waves of the incoming tide, blotting out Milton Ness at the top end of St Cyrus Bay. At their grandchildren's insistence our hosts ensured every dog went home with a special dogs' party goody bag – unbelievable really.

We made our way back to the cars telling each other what tremendous fun it had all been. The truth of the matter is it had been a howling success, and I'd do it again however barking mad anyone else should think I might be.

Days Here and There

We're home – the Doyenne and I, that is – after a short break in Aberdeenshire. We didn't go far, just a forty-minute drive over the Cairn o' Mount and into the Vale of Cromar. Since I was a child it has always been a bit of an adventure motoring up that long winding hill, and stopping at the summit to scramble up the Cairn and add another stone to the top for luck.

Crossing that summit from east to west takes you not only into another county but into its own microclimate. The hills form a barrier and you can leave one side in glorious sunshine and drop down the other into teeming rain – even snow. And the geography on either side is as different as chalk from cheese. Looking across Deeside, all you see are the Grampian hills marching westward like so many Roman legionaries. As the Doy-enne remarked – 'there are no flat fields in Deeside.' Our bedroom looked south, and each morning we were greeted by glorious vistas of hills and forests coming to life in the rising sun.

A rickle of gravestones, several hundred yards off the road, caught my eye and I just had to investigate. It's always fascinating to read who lived and worked and died in a place. Farms called Coldhome and Hardgate were aptly named and give an idea of the nature of the landscape, and of the kind of lives that the families, who worked the land, lived a hundred years ago and more.

We were surprised that in such a lonely spot the grass round the graves was all neatly cut and tidy. An absolutely plain building, without even the simplest bell-housing on the gable, gave no indication that this was the very ancient Migvie Kirk. A carved Pictish symbol stone standing at the entrance to the graveyard confirms the antiquity of the site which is dedicated to St Finan and dates back to the eighth century.

We pushed open the door expecting to see cobwebs and a few broken-down pews. We couldn't possibly have anticipated the sight that greeted us. As a memorial to his parents, the local laird the Hon. Philip Astor of Tillypronie, has restored the building and transformed the interior to a place of beauty and peace for quiet reflection.

Our initial reaction when we pushed open the door

and found the interior flooded with clever internal lighting was gasps of astonishment. The building has been completely stripped out to provide a canvas for the best skills of local artists as a celebration of the memory of Philip Astor's parents.

Three stained-glass windows depicting the local landscape, lit from behind, sing with colour. From outside they are just blank eyes giving no clue to their impact against the plain white walls inside. Panels with secular and biblical quotations from great and good men have been painted – apparently randomly, but I'm sure as part of a very thoughtful plan – to take the visitor on a journey of contemplation.

One supplicant begs, 'Oh Son of God, perform a miracle for me . . .' Perhaps it started in this unexpected place.

In the centre of the room four massive stone communion chairs sit round a communion table. A great cross, carved out of the plasterwork, imposes itself on the whole space. A mythical bird of prey and a travelling visionary (perhaps?), who may have visited the holy site, are depicted high up on the wall. If painting is a condition of the soul, the soul is stripped back to its essentials here.

Nor was the woodcarver forgotten. As a reminder of the eternal thread of life, the interlaced knot-work pattern of the Celtic cross on the eighth-century carved stone at the entrance to the graveyard has been reproduced on the inside of the double doors of the church. It would be a nice touch if the wood for them had come from the Tillypronie Estate on which the church stands.

Overawed is not a word to use lightly, but neither the Doyenne nor I came away wanting to talk about our experiences until we'd had time to gather our thoughts. It was a place we didn't want to leave. We didn't altogether understand the significance of some of the things we saw and read, but they were there for a reason. So we'll go back. This natural building encourages you to empty your mind and in the calming influence of its simplicity think about the value of our lives.

On the home journey the weather was clear and the view from the cairn, eastwards to the coast, was just stunning. To paraphrase (very badly!) the great Dr Samuel Johnson: 'the noblest prospect which an Angus loon ever sees is his home county spread out below him from the top of the Cairn o' Mount.'

And what of the dogs? There wasn't much coming over them while we were away, having their own little holiday in the local kennels. When I delivered them they greeted the kennel staff and bounded in with every anticipation of enjoying themselves. When I collected them they showed no signs of having missed us but bounded out again, smothering me in bad breath and moulting black hair, delighted to see the old familiar face. Beauty in a dog's life is probably the certainty of long walks and two square meals a day!

Science Finds, Industry Applies, Man Conforms

A 'Mowbot' sounds as though it might be faintly vulgar, but in fact it is the brand name of a robot motor-mower. I was bidden by a friend who received one for his birthday, no doubt in recognition of his advancing years and waning enthusiasm for cutting grass, to go and see his new toy in action.

About the size of a case of wine the little machine takes all the effort and tedium, mental as well as physical, out of one of summer's most boring garden chores. Powered by two rechargeable batteries it wanders across the lawn, apparently at random, but actually in response to signals from a wire buried round the edge of the grass.

The Mowbot has its own inbuilt computer and is programmed to start work every morning at 11 a.m. and continue unattended until 5 p.m. Its owner has built it its own little kennel (which is rather sweet!) and in the event of heavy rain two sensors on top of the lid direct it back to the refuge of its wee shelter.

Because it comes out to work every day the miniscule shaving, which it cuts, is mulched, so there's no worry about emptying a grass-catcher. You can leave home at ten o'clock in the morning and return after six confident that the grass has been cut. It's like having a dog which never makes a mess and doesn't need training! It provided quite one of the best excuses for sitting drinking tea – the sun had not passed the yardarm, so it was too early for gin and tonic – that I have come across for a long time.

It was not the first time my host has been dazzled by the appliance of science. The doyenne and I used to go sailing with him and his Doyenne on the west coast. The favourite piece of equipment on the boat was the electronic tiller pilot which steered the boat automatically, leaving both hands free to pour gin and tonic. This cunning little appliance was known as 'Komrade Pistoff', which I suspect was a pun based on the fact that it was powered by a pist**ON**. I know it's a joke in the worst possible taste, but then most puns are.

Big boys with big toys don't restrict themselves to garden and nautical gadgetry. A neighbour has discovered remote-controlled helicopters. He didn't quite master the controls to begin with and £40-worth of toy got stuck up a tall tree. Undismayed, he dashed out to buy a bigger, shinier model costing £250 which I fear may get stuck up an even taller tree. I suppose these things affect you like a drug. He'll have to have every new model and every gizmo that goes with it until one day he loses touch with reality. And I'll probably have to climb the tree to recover his helicopter.

Holidays in Scotland

The spiritual homeland of West Highland terriers must surely be the west Highlands of Scotland, so we hoped that our holiday in Ardnamurchan would be as west-Highlandy for Macbeth as it was possible to be.

We've just returned from a self-catering fortnight in the village of Kilchoan about six miles from the famed Ardnamurchan Lighthouse, the most westerly point on the mainland of Scotland. Kilchoan holds dramatic memories from the past. We first stayed there some thirty-five years ago. I took our daughter Cait, then aged four, to fish for poddlies (young coal fish) off the Mingarry pier. When my attention wandered Cait's did too, and I was brought sharply back to reality when she fell into the sea. The Doyenne was pretty tight-lipped about the whole event when we got back. We did go fishing again, but the children were firmly roped to the pier thereafter.

The Ardnamurchan Peninsula is a truly unspoilt part of Scotland – indeed it would be a pretty difficult task to spoil what is essentially one of our west-coast wilderness areas. Geologically it is very old, and agriculturally not suited to much more than sheep and deer. Near the shore are grass pastures which are separated from the sea by typical west-coast machair. Described as 'the land of the smiling, coloured flowers', the machair holds a great diversity of plant and bird life.

Sea pinks abound, as do clover, marsh marigolds, ragged robin, vetches, purple orchids, stonecrops, blue and white foxgloves and yellow flags, which always take me straight back to childhood holidays at Ullapool. And that's only touching on the paintbox of colour.

Walking on Sanna beach, which I consider to be

second only to Sandwood Bay in Sutherland, we saw dunlins and ringed plovers and were serenaded by skylarks. At the Glenmore Interpretative Centre we watched fledged heron chicks nearly ready to leave the nest. One memorable morning, out with the dogs, I spent an hour watching an otter swimming in the sea below ruined Mingarry Castle. In the background two cuckoos were calling. At night little pipistrelle bats hunted amongst the trees helping to keep the midge population down.

A regular car ferry operates between Mingarry and Tobermory. We spent a delightful day on Mull visiting the gardens at Torosay Castle. A community butcher's shop has been set up in Tobermory, run by and for the community. It means that farmers can avoid the cost of sending their beasts by ferry to the mainland for slaughter, consequently receiving a better profit for their endeavours. We took back with us a delicious leg of Mull lamb which gave us a memorable supper and cold cuts for the picnic next day.

It's a land of dwindling crofting communities amongst the dramatic hills and mountains. Every morning we woke to the sight of the sun on Beinn Talaidh (Talla), rising away to the south on Mull – except of course when it was obscured by traditional west-coast drizzle!

From the Doyenne's Kitchen

Most of us only know about razor clams, or razor shells, from the empty shells which look like old fashioned cut-throat razors littering the beaches. Son Robert has given me his special recipe for:

SPOOT FRITTERS

The colloquial term in Scotland for razor clams is 'spoots' (or spouts).

They are available, live, from good fishmongers wrapped in bundles and looking like a clutch of Cuban cigars with lolling 'tongues'. The tongues are part of the body of the clam that sticks out of the top of the shell. They are absolutely delicious and every shellfish connoisseur should try a razor clam at least once in their life. A bundle of spoots will feed two adults as a delicious main course, or four as a starter.

A bundle of spoots (live)
2 eggs '
1 oz fresh breadcrumbs
Salt
Pinch of cayenne pepper
Oil for deep frying
Salad leaves

Method

1. Rinse the spoots in cold water. It is a good idea to check them at this stage; similar to mussels, the shells should close and the body of the clam should return to its shell when handled.

2. Having rinsed and checked them, pop them in a pan of boiling water and boil gently for a couple of minutes to open the shells.

3. Now for the fiddly bit – strain off the water and retain the liquor. Strip out the clam meat from the shells. Chop it coarsely and put to one side. Discard any bits you don't like the look of.

4. Separate the eggs. Beat the yolks and stir in the chopped clam meat, the breadcrumbs and a wee bit of the liquor. Add salt and the cayenne pepper.

5. Whisk the egg whites until stiff and fold into the clam mixture.

6. Heat plenty of oil in a deep frying pan and when hot, deep-fry spoonfuls of the mixture a few at a time.

7. Remove the fritters when brown and crisp. Drain on kitchen paper to remove excess oil.

8. Serve with a good dry white wine and salad.

I've tried to fish for razor clams so as to have them even fresher, but so far they have eluded me. They are best gathered at the spring tides which are lower than the usual low tides. The expression is confusing because spring tides have nothing to do with the season but occur just after the full and new moons, uncovering more of the low tide sand than usual for this seashore foraging. The spoots bore into sand leaving a visible si-phon hole. The technique appears to be to pour a small quantity of cheap kitchen salt down the hole. Once salted they come hurtling to the surface and it is then a case of wrestling them from their sandy homes and whisking them back to the kitchen to prepare them.

JULY

Walks With a Grandson

Arcane agricultural occupations, red poppies, a history lesson, bottom eaters (really!), two dukes, bullish behaviour, castle speakeasy, bird chicks are learning to fly, pollen count is rising to the consternation of hay fever sufferers and the bearded barley is starting to ripen.

A Funny Way With Words

Tattie roguing is in full swing. This odd-sounding activity is essential to ensure that the potato crops being grown this season to provide next season's seed potatoes are disease free, and also free of 'rogue' or unwanted varieties that would adulterate the integrity of the intended crops. The early potatoes are already in flower – very colourful and providing acres of white or blue flowers (depending on variety) each with a deep orangey centre.

Squads of young men, and doubtless young women too, can be seen in the fields walking purposefully up the tattie dreels (the drills which separate the ridges) armed with garden forks to dig out any offending plants. Modern agricultural machinery is so powerful that the drills are all as straight as arrows. The raised ridges (like raised beds to ensure proper drainage), which the potatoes grow in, are much wider and taller than I remember when I was a youngster, and no doubt produce much larger crops.

We – the Doyenne and I, and dogs too – drove past a field at Westdrums Farm, near Brechin, which looked like a dusty blue-coloured carpet. It was a crop of linseed, or flax, and a hundred years or more ago would have been a common sight. Flax of course is the plant from which linen is woven and older readers will remember the linen mills (Webster's Mill in Arbroath was about the last), which grew up around the linen industry. Nowadays, the linseed is crushed for its oil and to make animal feed, although recently there have been trials run to see if it might be possible once more to grow flax commercially for linen, and revive an old trade which was once very prominent in the Angus area. Flax is a bonny blue colour, so you'd expect flaxen to be much the same. But no – flaxen is a bonny blonde colour. It's funny the way words go!

We've had some lovely sunny days recently and the dogs have lain out on the grass enjoying the warmth. It does Sheba no end of good to get the heat into her rheumaticky bones. Macbeth, who has as much brains as a docken, lies in the full sun panting like a steam engine and almost passing out before he drags himself into the shade of the hedge. While dogs do have sweat glands – they are in the pads of their feet – panting, to expel excess heat, is their primary way of regulating their body temperature and cooling down.

We have three tubs of wild strawberries which produce a couple of small pickings of fruit. Cut a galia melon in half, scoop out the seeds and fill the cavity with the strawberries. The contrast between the sweet melon and sharp zing of the berries is almost unbelievable. This is an offering fit for – well, a Doyenne. I'm just thankful melons come in two halves!

Affairs of Youth

The poet John Dryden wrote of 'youth, beauty, graceful action.' He might have had in mind the roe deer calf that was standing in the middle of the road as I came bowling round the corner. I expect it was one of two calves that I had seen grazing alongside their mothers when I was out with the dogs. They've grown out of the teenage awkwardness when their legs seem too long for their bodies, and have developed into the elegance of near maturity.

The calfie got a severe fright at the sudden appearance of the car, and bolted down the road looking for a break in the hedge. It soon scrambled through and no doubt spent the next little while pondering on the noisy monster that was the latest addition to its short life experience.

As I drove round the next corner I was confronted by a very junior red squirrel running down the centre of the road towards me. I braked, but it seemed quite oblivious of the car. I often see them feeding close to the roadside so perhaps they just get complacent about these noisy animals that tear past at such unseemly speeds.

This one stopped, sat back on its hind legs and gazed at me for several moments, then shot beneath the hedge. I watched it climbing up and round the trunk of a beech tree until it disappeared from view.

Brave Mother

The Doyenne and I took ourselves, and Macbeth of course, off for a day's diversion in Aberdeenshire. We took the familiar route by the B974 over the Cairn o' Mount and stopped to look back. The Cairn is one of the historic mountain passes and drover roads across the foothills of the Grampian Mountains, linking Deeside with the Howe of the Mearns and the coastal plain of south Kincardineshire. In the seventeenth and eighteenth centuries it was one of the main routes from the north to the cattle sales.

Eastwards from its 1,500 feet summit we were looking at Montrose Bay and the North Sea, and the white pencil of Scurdie Ness Lighthouse guarding the entrance to Montrose Harbour. With the binoculars we picked out the farms and houses of friends and neighbours, but we were headed westwards and we got on our way again dropping down into Deeside and Aboyne. Turning right at Dinnet we headed into the hinterland by Logie Coldstone.

We had our picnic by the side of a loch. The sun popped out intermittently as we watched several families of tufted duck, seven or eight ducklings in each, paddling around the fringes of the reeds. They are one of our commonest diving ducks and the youngsters were perfecting their techniques, diving below the surface and a few moments later popping back up like wee black corks.

A black-backed gull landed on the water beside one of the families. Duckling seemed to be top of the menu for lunch, but the mother bird was having none of it. She lunged angrily at the intruder, which took off smartly and didn't try to return.

Walks with a Grandson

It is so peaceful as the dusk deepens that the loudest noise is the sound of cattle in the field next door pulling at the grass as they feed. After about nine o'clock most birds have retired to roost, although the blackbirds are still chattering noisily amongst themselves and the swallows are busy catching daddy-long-legs and other airborne goodies to feed their young.

Our road is covered with sycamore wings, the V-shaped seeds which fall from the trees and spiral like mini-helicopters to the ground. These grand trees and the beeches, which were planted decades ago, form a leafy tunnel for cool walks with dogs. Their branches are so intertwined overhead that when it rains the leaves provide protection from all but the fiercest downpour.

I was given a bag of flounders, or 'flukes' as they are called locally, which I gutted and filleted. Lining the grill pan with kitchen foil the Doyenne grilled the fillets in melted butter and freshly squeezed orange juice and they were quite delicious. Usually regarded as a humble fish, much is in the cooking. She cooks lemon sole and dabs in the same way.

White blackbirds sometimes appear in the news because they are so uncommon. True albino blackbirds do occur I understand, but a piebald blackbird has appeared in our garden. When I was a youngster I was told that white feathers amongst the black are usually dead feathers resulting from an attack on the bird by a cat or suchlike. If this is true then our blackie must have had a hell of a tussle because there are white feathers all over its body. And, significantly perhaps, I have disturbed a large semi-feral looking cat prowling about in the garden and in the woods.

Grandson James and I took ourselves off on an exploration together and landed up sitting by the side of a pond. We watched the reflection of the clouds and the trees, and James commented that there was the whole world in the water – which was a wiser remark than he probably realised. Beneath the surface there's a teeming life cycle which we hardly see.

Fat cushie doos (wood pigeons) sat in the trees drugged with the heat of the sun, crooning away to themselves. Two flashing-winged birds were reflected in the pond. Mallard duck I thought, and looking above the tops of the trees I saw the birds speeding on. For me the highlight of our expedition was an electric blue dragonfly which hovered inches away from where we sat, quite still, so as not to disturb it. It's fun being a grandfather.

A Forfar reader telephoned to say that what we saw was more likely to be a damselfly as dragonflies are not particularly widespread in Scotland. I did some research and it seems likely that he was correct. Dragonflies flourish where there is healthy, clean water, indeed they can be said to be barometers of water quality. James and I were sitting beside a shallow, muddy-looking pool with heavily vegetated margins, which are ideal conditions for damselflies. So, on reflection I suspect that what we saw was an azure damselfly.

Don't Forget the Dogs

'Dogs die in hot cars' was the banner headline on the back cover of *The Big Issue*. I was much impressed that the magazine should be giving dog owners such a timely warning in the summertime. But, never assume! – it's actually the name of a Scottish band who are contemporaries of Franz Ferdinand. 'Pretty close to perfection,' they were described in the magazine.

It is a timely warning, however. It's no treat for dogs to be abandoned in a poorly ventilated and overheated car because owners get sidetracked with shopping or meeting friends. When you think about it, they wear their fur coats all year round in every sort of weather and temperature. In hot weather the inside of a car can heat up in minutes and your dog's body temperature will rise equally quickly to dangerous levels.

We've been working our way through the Doyenne's homemade elderflower cordial (the recipe for which appears in the first *Man with Two Dogs* book). Just as tasty as ever, and just the ticket when I've finished cutting the grass and need 'the tissues restored', as PG Wodehouse's Bertie Wooster would say. La D. has also made her first batch of strawberry jam with berries from Heughhead Farm near Friockheim, where they are grown to be picked and eaten in their proper traditional season. Granddaughter Cecily declared it to be 'yummy', so I suspect a couple of jars will go with her to Portknockie where the family will be spending their summer.

Red Poppies

Amongst my fund of 'utterly useless information' I have a note that the first patent for barbed wire was taken out in Ohio on 25 June 1867. Its modern development is called razor wire – for good reason, because it is absolutely lethal stuff. So far I've not seen the razor stuff used in an agricultural context but it all set me thinking about how necessary barbed wire really is. I phoned one of the wise farmers I know and got the answer.

There's still a very real need for barbed wire to control livestock. You'll see that the top strand, and occasionally the second one too, of most field fences are of barbed wire. Cattle will rub themselves against plain wire and slacken it, and fencing posts can get broken with the beasts' weight. Barbed wire discourages them and reduces maintenance. You won't see barbed wire on the lower strands, especially if there are sheep in the field. The wire would catch at the fleece, and that's a cash crop that needs to be safeguarded.

I've been out again with my strimmer cutting away and tidying up the tall grasses beneath the hedges. I leave this job till now because the grass has provided cover for young and newly-fledged birds, like thrushes and blackbirds, while they are still dependent on parent birds to feed them. They are also insect banks and an extra source of food. Macbeth too has had his regular summer strim. He goes in, as the Doyenne rather unkindly remarks, looking like a demented ball of string. The fragrant figure that emerges should be photographed for a chocolate box lid, if only we could keep him clean long enough.

On the way to Dundee, beside the bridge over the River South Esk at the Finavon Hotel (about halfway between Brechin and Forfar) I passed a field radiant with the yellow blossom of oilseed rape. What made it special were the poppies scattered throughout. In the sunshine, the yellow and scarlet and green of the vegetation could have been the inspiration for a Monet painting. I'd intended driving back home by the coast road, but I drove back to Brechin by the A90 again for the sheer pleasure of being able to enjoy the beauty of that field a second time. You have to make the most of nature's transient treats.

Historical Heroes

General Wade, whose memory is perpetuated in Wade's Bridges, was tasked by King George the First with taming the Highlands and the Highlanders after the unsuccessful 1715 Rebellion or Uprising (depending on which side of the historical fence you sit) led by Bonnie Prince Charlie's father, the Old Pretender. The General oversaw the construction of more than 250 miles of road and the completion of forty of his eponymous bridges. Facetiously nicknaming his road-

building soldiers his 'highwaymen', his building programme opened up the hitherto uncharted Highlands
and speeded up their eventual domination by the
English.

Last weekend was spent with kind friends who live
a stone's throw from the Old Bridge of Tilt, where it
crosses the River Tilt upriver from 'new' Bridge of Tilt.
This portion of the road and the bridge are part of the
original road north to Inverness, built by Wade's highwaymen. History breathed down our necks at every step.
This is Black Watch country, where our local Angus
and Perthshire regiment, the gallant FortyTwa, was
raised in 1739. Home, too, of the Atholl Highlanders,
Britain's only private army, commanded by the Duke
of Atholl.

It's a grand part of the country for dog walking and
we explored woodland tracks round Blair Castle and
into Glen Tilt. A poignant memorial is the stone at
the head of the glen marking the spot where James
Graham, Marquis of Montrose, raised the standard in
1644 on behalf of his sovereign, King Charles I. The
great Marquis is one of my historical heroes. He had
the courage to change his mind in support of his king.
H. V. Morton, in his second book of journeys through
Scotland, *In Scotland Again*, says it so well: '. . . Montrose
saw his duty clearly and, in his manner of fighting for it,
stands head and shoulders above every man of action in
the history of his country.'

In 1689 John Graham of Claverhouse, First Viscount
Dundee, a.k.a. Bonnie Dundee, or Bluidy Clavers

(depending on which side of the historical fence you sit), won the Battle of Killiecrankie leading the Jacobite forces supporting King James VII of Scotland and II of England against William of Orange's government troops. The Viscount was cut down in the early minutes of the battle, and died on open ground above the steep sides of the River Garry, which the River Tilt joins at Blair Atholl several miles up from the battle site. Although it was a stunning victory it had little overall effect on the outcome of the war, for the Jacobites had lost their brilliant leader and the highland clans loyal to James were routed a month later at the Battle of Dunkeld.

Perthshire is rightly called 'big tree country'. I believe it was the sixth Duke of Atholl who had his foresters fire cannonballs filled with seeds in order to plant trees on the most inaccessible cliff faces on his estate. Now they provide an ideal habitat for red squirrels. I noticed that the fur of Atholl squirrels is a darker tan than the rufous red of our local ones.

Literary Heroine

It's strange what sometimes triggers off these Saturday pieces. This week it was the phrase, 'the sma' licht', which appears in a Violet Jacob short story called *The Yellow Dog*, written very much in the Angus vernacular. Despite being born into one of the great 'county' families of her time, she had a familiarity with the daily, domestic language of country folk. The 'sma' licht' is the late gloaming when there's still a glimmer of light left in the evening sky. Not enough to read a newspaper by, but enough still to be able to recognise detail.

I realised how imperceptibly the nights are starting to draw in. Even a fortnight ago it never really got dark – the sma' licht effectively lasting throughout the night. The birds' evening chorus finally closed down around eleven o'clock and chimed up again about half past three of the morning.

Next month we'll be into the hairst (the harvest). I wonder what Violet Jacob would make of today's farm-ing methods and machinery? Compared with her day the countryside is empty and depopulated; the result of mechanisation. There's less to write about for it was the worthies and the characters, and her depiction of them, that bring her stories so much to life.

Thankfully nature, and the dogs, go about their affairs as busily as ever, providing me with an endless source of stories and comments for this weekly diary. Out with the Doyenne for their evening walk, Inka brought back to her an intact pheasant egg, which he dropped into her hand. It's called having a 'soft mouth', and hope-fully it's an indication of his general temperament.

We – the Doyenne and I, that is – were halted in our tracks by a small, determined hedgehog proceeding in a westerly direction up the middle of the highway. He stopped too, gazing long and hard at the car and deciding that, as his mother hadn't warned him about such noisy monsters, it was the better part of valour on his part to move to the side of the road.

There's a belief, built up through children's stories I think, that you can encourage hedgehogs to stay in your garden by leaving out bread soaked in milk. It seems that this is the worst thing you can do, however, as the mixture gives them diarrhoea which can lead to death.

Bottom Eaters

As with so many things, it's not what you know it's who you know. The mackerel have arrived at this part of the coast again and a neighbour has presented us with fresh fish caught off the rocks with rod and feather lures. My mother was rather snooty about mackerel, saying they were scavengers and fed off the bottom of the sea – 'bottom eaters' she called them, and maybe it was the association of words that contributed to her aversion. But eaten as fresh as possible, 'from pier to pan' as they say, they are delicious.

Once I've cleaned them the Doyenne cuts several deep slashes in the dense flesh to ensure they cook right through, and pops them under the grill. Because they are naturally so oily they don't need brushed with oil like most other whole fish. They have a robust taste which our whole family are very partial to. We took half a dozen with us to an impromptu barbecue organised by son Robert. Perhaps it was our imagination, but grilled outdoors they tasted even better. Like salmon and herring, mackerel are rich in omega-3 fatty acids which benefit the health of the heart.

My father built himself a sixteen-foot dinghy at the end of the Second World War which he kept at Ferryden, just across from Montrose Harbour. When I was a youngster he took me out in it to fish for the mackerel when they arrived in Montrose Bay each summer. I remember that they came in such great numbers that we would hear them banging their heads on the bottom of the boat.

At that time (the 1950s) Montrose Infirmary was independently run by a Board of Trustees and my father, who was a solicitor in the town, was the Clerk to the trustees. Sometimes he and I caught so many mackerel that he presented them to the Matron for the patients' tea. Looking back I wonder what the Matron thought of such a gift and whether the fish weren't surreptitiously dumped.

The Fish Man

A kipper for my tea on a summer's evening dislodged a memory that has lain dormant for an age, for kippers and summer holidays are subliminally entwined in my subconscious.

The best kippers I ever tasted were smoked by The Duke, in Ullapool. 'Aha!' I hear you say – 'another instance of seeing the past through rose-tinted spectacles.' Not a bit of it, I have my sister's recollections to back me up.

For seven years, from 1949, the family holidayed not quite in Ullapool itself but at Leckmelm Farm some three miles south of the village (as it was then; it's grown into a substantial town now). My father parked our caravan beside the pier that served the estate in the old days, nearly at the head of Loch Broom.

Kippers in those days were a proper man's meal. They overflowed the grill pan and overflowed the plate and my mother had problems cooking them on the caravan's small Calor gas cooker. No colouring or dye was used in the curing and what came out of the smokehouse was a golden-fleshed feast of thick, juicy fish meat that just needed heating through.

The Duke was an interesting character. He had been a master tailor in London and had been lucky to be pulled, more dead than alive, out of a building which was bombed in the blitz during the Second World War.

He recovered but was left with a withered arm and the doctors advised him to find an activity which would exercise the limb and restore its mobility.

Quite how he landed up in Ullapool from London, with wartime travel restrictions, I never knew. But he got there and, heeding his doctor's advice, took up fishing. Every morning he rowed a dinghy out into Ullapool Bay and threw a hand line over the side. He exercised his injured arm by lifting and dropping the fishing line so that the bait on the hook was in constant motion to attract fish.

I know he recovered enough mobility in the injured arm to lift a glass because, to my mother's constant irritation, my father and he spent many a happy hour in the public bar of the Caledonian Hotel whiling away the whisky. I don't think he ever left Ullapool, and the rest is kipper lore. He didn't lose his tailoring skills. He offered to make both Father and Mother 'fore and afters', or deerstalker hats. He took two measurements – a piece of string round the head, and another piece of string from ear to ear. The hats were produced in a couple of days, and worn with a fair degree of pride I have to say.

I don't know what happened to my father's hat, but we still have my mother's. It's probably the only hat, remaining in existence, made by The Duke. And there's one other thing, I never knew his real name.

Eat Up Your Psychedelic Vegetables

A 'carrot' tail I read on a Westie website, is a characteristic of a singularly well-bred West Highland white
terrier. Having just had his summer clip Macbeth's
profile (for the time being!) is still pretty clean-cut, and
as he trots on ahead of me on our walks it's surprising
how like a well-formed, white carrot his tail appears.

In the past it was common for terriers like Westies to
have their tails docked and, while docking is now generally banned in Scotland, we are thankful his breeder
decided to leave his tail intact anyway. The complete
item gives him a balance and urbanity which rounds off
his good looks. And that's quite enough high praise for
one small dog.

I've not seen white carrots on the plate, but I have
been hearing about purple carrots. They are packed
full of antioxidants and therefore doubly good for
us. When we were young my mother insisted my sister
and I ate up all our carrots because they helped us see
better in the dark. I have worn spectacles since I was
thirteen years old so Mother's homespun wisdom has
always been taken with a pinch of salt. Last summer
we bought purple cauliflowers which we chopped into
florets and served up raw with a dip, and they were
delicious. We had friends in for drinks who hadn't
come across this particular variety and didn't realise it
was their natural colour, and thought we must have
dyed them!

Sitting in the sunshine outside the back door, the peace was disrupted by Inka excitedly dashing across the drive and scenting around in the undergrowth. He had found a hedgehog which was none too pleased at being disturbed. I called Inka off and went back to finish my mug of coffee. I looked again some five minutes later expecting to see Mrs Tiggiewinkle still rolled up in a ball waiting for the excitement to die down. But with Inka out of the way she had wisely slipped away to a safe part of the woods, so discreetly and so quietly I hadn't noticed.

Feeling a Bit Bullish

'Bellowing like the bulls of Baal' is a description of extreme, intemperate noise – a 'beastly' noise, you might say. Baal was one of the ancient Egyptians' most important gods, rider of the clouds and god of fertility, who presided over not just the earth but the animals too. The bull was Baal's cult animal and symbol of the god's power.

Since the start of June our neighbours in the fields beside the house have been three bulls and their harem of cows. Perhaps it's the gods who decree that fertility must be saluted with bellowing. We're scarcely aware of it in the daytime, but throughout the nights the bulls have bellowed and groaned and grunted as nature has taken its course.

Walking past them with the dogs, the cows have seemed signally unimpressed with these passionate outbursts, ruminatively chewing their cud as they awaited their turn in this bovine rutting. We should start to see the outcome of their conjugal encounters sometime around 7 March next year, as I'm told cows have a gestation period of nine months and nine days.

Nostalgia

A great bush of yellow honeysuckle brightens up the approach to Edzell from Brechin. I stopped and cut a handful of the flowers to take home, for the scent of honeysuckle is the most nostalgic scent I know. Turning up the Glenesk road there are more bushes by the roadside. So I cut another handful and had them all in a vase for the Doyenne's return. We'll enjoy the fragrance throughout the house and, of course, it tops up the credit points with the Doyenne which is never a bad thing.

One Over the Excise Man

Old (long-standing, naturally) friend Dr Andrew Orr, retired from general practice and now filling his days by going down to the sea in boats, invited me out for a morning's fishing. The Doyenne's parting instructions were 'mackerel for supper, please.'

We drifted off St Cyrus beach and romantic sounding Tangleha' and, with the engine switched off, sat in companionable peace just talking when the mood took us. Andrew had seen the dolphins as we drove down the brae into Johnshaven, the small and historic Kincardineshire harbour where he keeps his boat. In the eighteenth century it was one of the largest fishing communities on the east coast of Scotland. Changes in fishing methods, transport, the people and their willingness to follow such a hard way of life has reduced the fishing to mostly part-timers creel fishing for lobsters and crabs, as is the case in the other small harbours up and down the coast.

I was delighted, once we were out on the water, to see the dolphins leaping in spectacular unison off the point at Milton Ness. I hoped they might have been attracted by the sound of the engine and swum over to investigate us, but no such luck. In earlier centuries the village of Miltonhaven is reputed to have been a free port, which meant that the lairds of nearby Lauriston Castle could land goods there without paying taxes or excise duty. The village was swept away in a fearful storm in 1795 and the township of Tangleha' grew up in its place. It would be a bit of a wheeze if the current laird, in a spirit of investigative research, landed several hogsheads of brandy at the small harbour to test the story. I'd look forward to drinking his health in the brandy – after I'd visited him in the clink, of course!

The Doyenne got her mackerel, and we ate them for supper that evening accompanied by a gift of red Duke of York potatoes which we steamed, rather than boiled, to retain their floury consistency. And a second picking of wild strawberries has been ripening in the troughs so I'll be able to give her another wee treat tomorrow morning.

Revisited

Spur of the moment decisions are often the best ones. Last Sunday seemed to herald in summer properly at last, so the Doyenne and I bundled the dogs into the car and set off to find new places to walk. We took the road from Edzell to Fern and Noranside, and eventually to Kirriemuir. It was a sunny day and a brisk, warm wind kept the clouds scurrying high across the sky. The countryside sparkled and the views were perfect in every direction.

I was all for driving over the road which splits the Caterthuns (Brown Caterthun and White Caterthun, two Iron-Age hilltop forts lying several miles north of Brechin) and continues down to the Bridge of Lethnot over the West Water. However, the Doyenne suggested taking the roadie just after Tigerton (pronounced 'Tigger-ton' as in A. A. Milne's *Winnie the Pooh* stories) which cuts into the hills at Kirkton of Menmuir. I've passed that road-end dozens of times but it had been ages since I'd driven over it. There's nothing special about it, just fields on each side. But as you crest the brae look a wee bit to the right and you see the gateway to Glen Esk. A wee bit to the left and you're looking at the back hills of Glen Lethnot.

We chose Lethnot. At the end of the road, at Waterhead, a track carries on up the Water of Saughs to the head of the glen. In all the times I've walked in Lethnot I'd never gone up that track, but the dogs and I have remedied that now.

I so enjoyed that walk that on Tuesday I chucked the dogs into the back of the car again, took my lunch piece and drove off once more to Lethnot. In the past, I've maybe not given it the credit it is due, but these two days I saw the glen looking its very best. I stopped in the heart of the glen and sat with the dogs beside the West Water – the sky was right, the clouds were right and great purple patches of bell heather glowed on the hillsides. The sun beat down like it was the real tabasco, and Macbeth got so hot I thought he would blow a gasket!

We looked down on a brown, peaty pool. At the head of it, the stream was broken by two rocks round which the water flowed before tumbling in a three-pronged cascade of white water, for all the world just like a grouse's claw. Fingerling-sized trout poppled the surface as they rose to feed on bugs and beasties blown off a silver birch on the opposite bank.

I wonder how many folk notice the grouse butt tucked into the side of the road as they drive home down the glen. It obviously hasn't been used for ages (you can't discharge a shotgun now so close to a public highway), but it's a wee work of art of the gamekeepers' drystane dyking skills.

From the Doyenne's Kitchen

Everyone is familiar with the saying 'Poacher turned gamekeeper', but until I met David Paterson I'd never met a gamekeeper turned chef. David was brought up in Edinburgh's historic port of Leith and, from early childhood, was taught to cook by his Italian mother. After a false start at catering college to train as a chef he joined the armed services. On completion of his service he became a gamekeeper and worked on several estates, latterly on the Gannochy Estate near Edzell. His passion for cooking rekindled itself and he returned to college to finish his chef's training. He is chef at The Burn, Edzell, a Georgian mansion at the foot of Glen Esk, now used as an academic centre for reading parties and study groups.

The wheel has turned full circle for David as he is back again in the part of north Angus where he worked as a gamekeeper. It seemed fitting to ask him to contribute a recipe to the book and the family have all given the thumbs-up of approval to:

THE BURN TOMATO CHUTNEY

3 lb ripe tomatoes
2 lb green apples
1.5 lb sultanas
2 oz salt
1.5 pints vinegar
2 teaspoons ground ginger
10 oz brown sugar
Juice of one lemon

Method

Slice the tomatoes. Core and slice the apples and put them with the remainder of the ingredients into a large heavy-based pan. Stir the mixture.

Place on the heat and bring to the boil. Simmer for approximately one hour until the mixture becomes thick and has turned a dark brown colour.

Spoon the mixture into hot sterilised jars and seal whilst still hot.

Makes about 4 lbs of chutney and is an ideal accompaniment to a strong mature cheese, and also hot or cold meats at summer barbecue meals.

AUGUST

Bonny Blooming Weather

Macbeth plays Macbeth; how smoked salmon gets onto our plates; hungry wasps and Sheriff soup; can't wait till Christmas; the whiff of whiffenpoofs; burrowing bees; walking on the water; singing mushrooms and wild fruits; the Jesus book. Hunt for sea anemones, crabs and other shellfish. The month for purple heather.

Up the Glen

Bright skies and shining sun were too good to miss, so Macbeth and I took ourselves off to one of the favourite walks up Glen Esk.

Just before I parked the car my attention was caught by tremendous house martin activity. Three of their familiar mud nests had been built under the lintel of a farmhouse window, and a pair were feeding chicks in one of them as others wheeled round and round taking little or no notice of me. They twisted and dipped in the air so fast that I couldn't tell how many of them there were, but it was a joy to sit and watch them for several minutes.

I was hoping to find wild mushrooms, but either someone had been there before me or it was a poor season for them because I didn't find one. I kicked at what I thought was a piece of orange peel that someone had carelessly dropped. It turned out to be a toadstool which I popped into the bag and brought home to identify. From the book it looks as though it is a fungus called 'orange peel' – so I was half right.

It was ideal weather for walking. Cotton wool clouds were high in the sky and the wind was cool but not cold. Macbeth was all over the place in pursuit of tantalising scents and got overheated and sounding like a wheeze-box. So we walked downhill to a stream where he stretched himself out in the shallows to cool.

We walked back up the hill and sat beside an abandoned cottage. I tossed a pebble onto the roof and more than a dozen rock pigeons erupted from the empty windows followed by another family of house martins. Their conspicuous white rump makes them the easiest of the swallow family to distinguish in flight. It was good to see them because they are not nearly so common in these parts as swallows are.

I watched the hillsides round about me, darkened by the shadows of the clouds as they passed over the sun. Close by a grasshopper noisily rubbed its rear legs together. I only recently discovered that this is called 'stridulating' – writing this column has fairly broadened my horizons! I have memories (I hope not figments of my imagination) of hearing grasshoppers all over the glen, but it's rare to hear one now.

Following Macbeth's example I stretched out on the short turf, cropped close by sheep and rabbits, and dozed in the warmth of the sun for fully half an hour. The only evidence of Man's imprint on the landscape was the deserted cottage with its dilapidated outbuildings, and ribbons of drystane dykes threading across the hills. A jet plane passing overhead, miles high, jogged me back to my other more mundane world, and Macbeth and I set off back to the car.

Pathfinding

Macbeth shall never vanquish'd be until
Great Birnam wood to high Dunsinane Hill
Shall come against him.

Words from *Macbeth*, Will Shakespeare's Scottish play, the play 'whose name cannot be spoken!' We were looking up at the summit of Dunsinane Hill, one of the Sidlaw Hills range, which marches between Perth and Dundee. An information board at the roadside told the story of Macbeth's Castle, the remains of which can be clearly traced amongst the thistles on the hilltop.

The meeting between old and new Macbeth might have been fateful, but a notice on the 'kissing gate' into the field, said 'No Dogs' – which was understandable as there were sheep in it. From new Macbeth's perspective, (which is pretty low-slung) it was just another heather-topped hill. He's not fond of heather; much of the time he can't see over it, it's hard going for a dog with such short legs and it scratches his stomach!

The Doyenne and I were escaping from the work party organised by son Robert to help him and his family move into their new home near Perth. We reckoned our best contribution to the day was taking grand-children Fergus and Cecily, and other grandson James, off 'pathfinding' (a long-established Whitson tradition) while the grown-ups got on with the hard work!

Historic Dunsinane is not a high hill, but it's steep. From the top it's easy to see why it was such a strate-gically good site for a fortress. There are clear views in every direction to spy the approaching enemy, and there is evidence that it was a place of defence as early as 1000 BC.

As the crow flies you're not far from the River Tay. The two bridges at Dundee straddling the River Tay and the summit of Dundee Law were all clearly visible. To the south, the Lomond Hills overlooking Loch Leven were in fine relief. Ali and Lenka from the Czech Republic had climbed the hill the previous week and left a message written in marker pen on a stone on the hilltop cairn. We wondered if they were seasonal agri-cultural workers taking time out from berry picking to sup up some of Scotland's darker history.

Birnam, next door to Dunkeld, lies fifteen miles westwards in the foothills of the Grampian Mountains.

Tradition says that Malcolm Canmore, who chased Macbeth out of his hilly fastness and eventually killed him to claim the Scottish throne as King Malcolm III, ordered his men to cut down branches from the Forest of Birnam in order to camouflage the size of his army. You'd think there might have been sufficient woodlands a lot nearer to Dunsinane to supply the attackers' needs.

I wonder if Malcolm Canmore, as he panted and peched up the hill, weighed down with his branch from Birnam, would have shared three-year-old Fergus' thought. 'Look at the view,' he announced, 'you can see for years.' I worry in case there's a hidden philosophy in that innocent remark that my cluttered adult mind has failed to connect with.

Wild Salmon

The Pullar family who own and operate the salmon netting station at Fishtown of Usan, just south of Montrose, go out twice a day throughout the course of the fishing season in their traditional salmon co-bles (high-prowed, open wooden fishing boats around twenty-seven feet long) to harvest the salmon from the bag nets. By comparison with the arrowhead-shaped jumper nets, which are anchored on the sandy shore between the high water mark and just below the low water mark, the bag nets are set permanently in deep water off the rocky shore between the Fishtown and

Ethiehaven at the south end of Lunan Bay, which was once a thriving fishing community of line fishers and salmon netters. The fishermen's cottages lie at the foot of cliffs, practically in the sea itself, and have all now been converted into holiday cottages and weekend retreats. The bag nets, like all methods of coastal salmon netting, are an ancient method of fishing which has changed little in its essential method over several centuries, although nets and ropes are now manufactured from polypropylene and other man-made fibres.

There's something of a family dynasty at Usan. Grandfather David, sons George and David junior, and grandsons John and Kevin are all involved in the business. I phoned to see if they would take two passengers, me and our own grandson James, out with them to watch them empty the nets. It would be a story for James to tell his friends when he gets back to school. As instructed we were on the beach on a lovely calm evening at eight o'clock sharp, ready to board the boat. It was a pleasure to see James's excitement as we left the mooring and motored to the head of Lunan Bay and the first net to be emptied.

The coble is brought alongside the submerged net, and the 'bag', which the salmon have swum into, is hauled on board. A rope fastener is pulled which opens the 'door' and the salmon fall into the boat and are quickly despatched. The door is tied up again and the net dropped back into the water to await the next catch on the next tide.

This is no nine-to-five job and it's not one for the faint-hearted. Depending on the tides which govern when the nets are emptied, the working hours are frequently unsocial. The netsmen must be prepared to go out whatever the weather, which is no respecter of their feelings. In summertime it may feel like a holiday but conditions can sometimes be so bad that they are prevented from getting to the nets, and damage to nets and gear from bad weather and heavy seas can be expensive.

This year (2005) they have been plagued with jellyfish; the big reddy-brown ones that you'll see stranded on the beach, waiting for the tide to come in and take them out to sea again. The jellyfish manage to swim into the nets and they fall into the boat along with the salmon. As the fish flap around in the boat they throw up pieces of stinging jellyfish tentacles and you need to protect your face and eyes – or suffer!

One hundred salmon and grilse (smaller salmon weighing up to about six pounds) were landed that evening. They were graded and packed into boxes with ice. Within hours they were on their way to the London market.

James was given three sea bass which had also found their way into the nets to take home for his grandmother's tea. Until recently these fish were found primarily in the southern waters of the UK. With the increase in North Sea summer temperatures owing to climate change and global warming they are now a quarry fish for the sea anglers – but, happily for James, not for the salmon netsmen.

Paper Houses

This week's piece comes from the Borders where the Doyenne and I are visiting son James and his family. They live in a secret, out-of-the-way corner, five miles from Peebles. It's well off the main road, so quite safe for grandchildren to race about in total freedom. Their unusual house was built very much with sustainability in mind, of an all-wood construction and with shingle tiles.

Their garden has been a delight – it's full of butterflies, which we seem to see fewer and fewer of in our own garden. It's not until you see them again in some numbers that you realise how much you've missed them. Red admirals, peacocks and large whites feed on borders of scabious and catmint. Honey bees from the hives in both James's garden and his neighbour's feed on clumps of white globe thistles. Bumble bees, which are under threat in our countryside, are also attracted to the thistles' nectar.

Their neighbour Wendy pointed out a perfect example of nature's mimicry. A hover fly had assumed the markings of a bumble bee, and at a casual glance it was easy to mistake it for one. It had the bumbler's distinctive yellow stripe on its rump but the giveaway, if you are an entomologist like Wendy, is the eye shape and the antennae.

She also told me about wasps scraping minute, wasp-sized bites of wood from the walls of the house, which they chew to make the paper with which they make their bikes. James has heard them, in very calm conditions, munching away at his home! Because we regard wasps as pests and swipe at them with rolled-up newspapers, we forget to wonder how they make their extraordinary nests. I have very carefully (for they are so fragile) cut away a deserted one from the ceiling of a shed and broken it open. It really is another of nature's miracles how such an apparently flimsy construction can be home and breeding chamber to such large numbers of insects.

Illegal Soup

Looking out to sea you could be forgiven for thinking nothing interesting happens out there, but ask grandson James and he'll tell you a different story.

Kind friends who have a boat invited James and me out on a fishing trip. It was a proper, sunny summer's afternoon after the interminable rain we've endured all through July. They keep their boat at Johnshaven, a harbour I remember well as I kept a boat there myself for several years. We took a 'piece' with us to eat on board so that we could make the best of our time at sea.

It's funny how things turn up again – it was just last month that I wrote about the mackerel we were given which brought back childhood memories. I like the idea that James will have happy memories of his first experience of sea fishing and catching mackerel. Hopefully they will stay with him and be passed on to his own children, and his grandchildren after. At his age, when grandfather arranges a fishing trip grandfather is expected to come up with the goods. I felt under some pressure, but thankfully our friends know the likely fishing spots and young Mr Smug returned home with six fish to my one.

With the aid of modern communications and his mobile phone, the Doyenne had news of James's success before we landed. There's not much you can teach an experienced grandmother and by the time we got home she was making gooseberry sauce (a traditional accompaniment to mackerel) from gooseberries we'd picked the evening before from bushes that had seeded wild in an old beech hedge. We sat down at the kitchen table to a special meal of fish, provided free by our grandson, and gooseberries, picked for free from a hedgerow. There're worse places to be than the countryside.

Out from Johnshaven harbour and looking back to land you can see what remains of the old stump of the Kaim of Mathers clinging to the cliff top just north of the sands of St Cyrus Bay. The Kaim (castle) has connections with a gruesome murder worthy of the talents of Hammer films. David Barclay of Mathers built the fortress to escape the wrath of King James I after he and three neighbouring lairds brutally murdered the local Sheriff, James Melville of Glenbervie. The lairds' repeated complaints to him about the Sheriff's heavy-handed behaviour so exasperated the king that, without thinking, he said, 'Sorrow gin he were sodden and supped in bree.' In other words, for all he cared they could go and make soup of the Sheriff.

So they did. At the aptly named 'Sheriff's Kettle' they tipped the ill-starred lawman into a huge cauldron, and boiled him up – and supped the bree! You'll not find a recipe for this in the Doyenne's cook book but doubtless the incident represented a fifteenth-century version of a picnic. Nowadays Sheriffs lead more serene lives . . . !

A Whiff of Whiffenpoofs

The hairst, or harvest time, is the culmination of every farmer's year when he learns how successful all the hard work of previous months has been. Combine harvesters are in the fields as farmers push on to get their barley cut before the next downfall of rain. And tattie harvesters, like great red monsters, crawl along the narrow roads journeying from field to field to lift the potato crop. We'll not see our neighbours for several weeks until their crops are safely in and secure from bad weather.

The last picking of raspberries wasn't really fit for the table so I used the fruit to make raspberry vodka. I needed a recipe and phoned a friend whose instincts in these matters I knew I could trust. It's quite simple – just raspberries, vodka and sugar in the right quantities. And then comes the hard bit. I have to wait at least till Christmas for the mysteries and chemistry to complete their magic. In the meantime I'm giving the bottles a good shaking every other day or so to mix all the ingredients and ensure the brew is in peak condition for a Hogmanay toast.

Like many others, when the word got out I hot-footed it up to Cortachy at the foot of Glen Clova to get a sighting of the whiffenpoofs. This was a first appearance so far north and there was no knowing if they would come back again in my lifetime. No one could say if their arrival at this unlikely spot was another result of global warming, or whether they had been blown off course by high winds in their migration across the Atlantic.

Shy creatures, they were slow to make an appearance straight away, but the wait was worth it. Their distinct plumage of long black tails and white breasts was reminiscent of the magpies of their eastern American homeland, and they had a remarkable range of exotic and tuneful call-notes. They are obviously social birds and there was some discussion whether their singing was to defend their territory or attract females.

I'm afraid I'm being rather frivolous. The reality is that The Whiffenpoofs from America's Yale University are the oldest collegiate, unaccompanied, *a cappella* group in the US. As part of their annual singing tour they appeared at Cortachy Castle (at the foot of Glen Clova north of Kirriemuir, hometown of Peter Pan's creator J. M. Barrie) and for over an hour they entertained an enthusiastic audience.

The group's wide range of voices matched their wide repertoire of songs from Cole Porter to Johnny Cash and their signature 'Whiffenpoof Song' with its chorus adapted from Rudyard Kipling's poem, 'Gentlemen Rankers'. The castle setting was ideal for their formal white tie and tails presentation, and the singers' pleasure in making music together was very evident. And the audience loved it all.

Much is written about the dawn chorus, but when the concert finished and we strolled back to the car in the fading evening light, we enjoyed a dusk chorus to equal anything heard in the half light of early morning.

Father's Memory

Come in ahint, ye wan'erin' tyke!
Did ever a body see yer like?
Wha learnt ye a' thae poacher habits?
Come in ahint, ne'er heed the rabbits!
Noo bide there, or I'll warm yer lug!
My certie! ca' yersel' a doug?

These are the opening lines of 'Dandie', a poem from a small collection of the same name, written by W. D. Cocker, which I came across in the bookcase. I can't remember buying it myself, but it was the sort of wee book my father would have bought. He was a great one for vernacular poetry.

It has survived several flittings (house removals) without coming to light before and, now that I've found it, I've thoroughly enjoyed Mr Cocker's poetry. He must have lived somewhere over East Dunbartonshire way for he writes about Kippen, and about Strathendrick and Endrick Water in the Campsie Fells.

Another poem is entitled 'A Covenanter'. The non-conformists or Covenanters were very strong in south-west Scotland. They had covenanted amongst themselves to maintain Presbyterianism in Scotland and defied King Charles I's attempts to impose Episcopacy. Their defeat latterly by government forces was largely due to the leadership of John Graham of Claverhouse, Viscount Dundee – 'Bluidy Clavers' to his enemies.

Perhaps the poet was a farmer, because Dandie was a young sheepdog. As soon as I read the lines I thought of Macbeth. He's certainly a 'wan'erin' tyke' and he has poacher habits, too. If I don't keep my eye on him as we pass the rhododendrons where the rabbit burrows are he's in there like a shot, out of sight, and then there are several minutes of ineffectual threats and shouting. Many's the time I could warm his lug. But he knows his man, and as I reach a crescendo he comes creeping out shaking himself and wagging his tail as if to say, 'They'll not trouble you again today.'

This article brought an e-mail from a reader who had met Mr Cocker:

> I was just a wee lad at the time but he had tea at our house before my father took him along to our church Men's Club where (he) was the guest speaker. Like yourself we have always had a copy of *Dandie and other Poems* on our bookshelves. I remember asking him to sign our copy when he visited and I still have it.

Burrowing Bees

Monday afternoon – walking with the dogs in the baking afternoon sun the dusty bank ahead of us seemed to be moving with ants scurrying all over it, and I thought we had stumbled on a nest. I kept the dogs to heel (the last thing I wanted was hordes of the insects running amuck in Macbeth's thick coat) but as we got closer it was clear they were airborne and quartering the area just above ground level.

Closer inspection showed that they were small bees, similar to honey bees, and some were crawling in and out of tiny holes in the earth. Inka was snapping at them, trying to catch them in mid-flight. I soon pulled him away too. Heaven knows what would have happened if he'd got one up a nostril! I phoned a bee man who told me I'd discovered a colony of miner bees, so called because they burrow into the soil where they lay their eggs.

The bee man's explanation for the low-flying activities was to create currents of air to cool down the vicinity of the hive and stop the larvae from overheating. The ones entering the holes would have been taking moisture inside for the same reason.

Tuesday morning – 5.30 a.m. to be precise – I was woken by a clatter of thunder, followed almost instantly by torrential rain. I could hear it dinging off the car roof and when I looked out of the window it was fair stottin' (to use a good nor'east expression) off the ground. Thunder and lightning and rain lasted for more than an hour and I worried about my miner bees.

My bold boys and I walked round by the hive to see what damage it might have suffered and were greeted by half a dozen sad-looking individuals drifting aimlessly around. I assumed the rest had been either washed out or drowned. I should have known better.

Wednesday morning dawned bright and warm and we took another turn round by the dusty bank – just to check. After millennia of bee experience and dealing with far worse weather than we'd experienced the previous day, the miner bees were out again in force enjoying the sunshine.

Maybe I've not been looking in the right places, but I've hardly seen any honey bees this year. Hopefully it's just a local blip because we enjoy our honey in this household. The blue delphiniums in the bed at the front of the house have been attracting the big, furry bumble bees we used to call 'foggy toddlers'. A smaller variety have been busy in the hedgerows gathering pollen and nectar. Earlier in the season I saw the red bum bees with rusty-coloured rear ends, affectionately nicknamed 'red arses'.

At the beginning of this week my practical knowledge of bees was pretty scanty. I know a bit more now.

Fungal Growths

The past four or five months seem to have scooted by. Being very busy anyway has concentrated my mind on other things, but it seems no time since the dogs and I were walking under bare trees waiting for that magic moment when the branches took on the whisper of green which heralded spring's first leaves.

Now it's harvest time again, but the prospects aren't good for farmers round here. There's been too much rain when they needed settled weather. I spoke to farmer Alex Sanger at Hillside, outside Montrose, who confirmed that some of the winter barley that was looking buttery ripe some three weeks ago is looking grey now because of repeated soakings. Oilseed rape, which has been cut, won't dry for the same reason. Even if it can be saved the quality and yield will be well down and barley that was destined for whisky malting (and a high price) will go for animal feed instead.

The sometimes torrential rain in recent weeks caused the river levels to rise and fall very rapidly, almost like flash floods. I spoke to an angler on the bank of the River North Esk who told me the river had fallen more than two feet in the time he and his companions had been on the water. (It's a quaint expression, when you think about it. Anglers are only 'in' the water if they fall in, otherwise they are 'on' it, which may indicate an arrangement with higher authority denied to the rest of us!)

Amongst the beech trees I've been finding chanterelle mushrooms which I gather first thing in the morning and bring home to fry up with streaky bacon. Kind friends who are away have invited us to invade their garden and use some of the vegetables which would otherwise go to waste. We are appreciating their tomatoes fresh off the vine, and broad beans which are quite delicious with crispy fried bacon mixed through them, smothered in a white parsley sauce. Somehow this seems the ideal way to garden.

The wet conditions have produced a terrific harvest of other multicoloured and misshapen mushrooms and toadstools. We had the four youngest grandchildren visiting last weekend and I was quite anxious about small hands picking up something very nasty. Thankfully they all seem to understand that pretty and colourful doesn't necessarily mean safe.

Musical Mice

Country mice sometimes go to town, which is what the Doyenne and I did recently. We usually try to take a short break during the Edinburgh Festival to sup up a bit of culture.

We heard a delightful piano recital of Mozart and Schubert in St George's and St Andrew's Church in George Street. This is a fine example of Georgian

New Town Edinburgh architecture – oval inside and beautifully decorated. Built to the glory of a god, it has the most wonderful acoustics for such an instrumental presentation and provided as great a celebration of a musical experience as any spiritual one.

There was no place for dogs, of course, who went to The Moorie Kennels at St Cyrus. It's always very gratifying when we go collect them to be told that they have been no trouble and that the kennel staff enjoy looking after them. We've been lucky with the dogs we've owned. One or two may have been fairly brainless (no names, no pack drill) but every one has had a thoroughly decent nature, which was terribly important when our family were small.

This season has been quite the best I can remember for wild raspberries and they have grown in great profusion. One afternoon I picked over five pounds, and because they are half the size of the cultivated fruit it took me twice as long. I bore them home proudly to the Doyenne who, despite having already made potfuls of raspberry jam, popped them in the jam pan and boiled them up for raspberry jelly.

For husbands like me who rarely question what goes on in the kitchen, I've discovered that jelly is made by boiling the berries until they dissolve into a red mush, which is strained through a muslin bag overnight (I'm told that in the bad old days a baby's Harrington nappy was used – well washed I hope) into a bowl. The Doyenne did magic things with the resultant bree and what I spoon out of the jam jar onto my toast is such a mouth-watering confection that I've begged her not to give any of it away.

Sometimes children innocently make remarks of such devastating candour that they have to be accepted in the spirit in which they are made. A little girl arriving at church without her hymn book electrified the congregation by announcing in piercing tones, 'Oh bugger, I've left my Jesus book behind!'

I can't help thinking that Jesus who, so the tale is told, was human enough to lose his temper with the money changers in the temple and overturned their tables, might have felt a twitch of sympathy for this youthful oversight. But the next time our granddaughter comes to stay we'll make jolly sure she has her hymn book firmly in her hand when we take her to our church.

Natural Harvest

Encouraging wildlife to the garden can be expensive. One way to do it is by planting the right flowers to attract bees and butterflies, and the right berry-bearing bushes and trees such as cotoneasters, rowans, geans (wild cherries), hollies and hawthorns for the bigger songbirds like the blackbirds. A cheaper way is to leave wild areas in corners of the garden where seed-ing thistles and other weeds can flourish and support tits and finches.

We are fortunate to have plenty of natural food sources for the wildlife round the house. Fallen, rotting trees provide breeding areas for insect life and the big bugs feed on the little bugs which they find in the composted undergrowth. In turn, they attract song thrushes and starlings which we watch foraging amongst dead leaves in their search for the insects sheltering below.

A myriad of fungi have appeared again this year and large numbers of the caps have been nibbled by mice and other small woodland rodents. In several months the pigeons will be feeding on the beech mast from the beeches which are so widespread.

Our major contribution to the food chain is peanuts. We have four feeders and our efforts have been repaid by five red squirrels (there may be more) and several families of woodpeckers that patronise us. Two strains of squirrel are evident. One has blonde, almost old-ivory coloured tails. We see three others scampering around the back green with brindled tawny and black-haired tails, each trying to outdo the others in their efforts to get most food.

There appear to be at least three families of wood-peckers that visit the canteen. However if the pressure on food gets too great the adults may chase this season's young birds away to fend for themselves further afield. It's quite common to see the two species feeding together, although the squirrels are definitely the dominant ones in the pecking order – if you see what I mean!

From the Doyenne's Kitchen

Our family and their spouses are all such excellent cooks that I am including some of their creative ideas. September in Scotland is the time for the autumn run of wild salmon returning to their mother rivers to spawn. You can tell the difference between harvested salmon and the wild fish. Daughter-in-law Harriet has given me her favourite recipe for salmon.

SIDE OF SALMON – THAI-STYLE

Whole side of salmon
Bunch of spring onions
5 crushed cloves of garlic
2 or 3 chopped red chillies
Half a small bottle of dark soy sauce
Juice and zest of 2–3 limes
4 tablespoons of runny honey
Big bunch of chopped fresh coriander
Salt to taste and lots of black pepper

Method

Mix all ingredients together and rub all over the salmon and leave to marinate for at least half an hour. Pre-heat the grill and grill the fish for 10–15 minutes, until crispy on top and still a bit pink in the middle. Keep a careful eye on it as the honey can burn quite suddenly! (When this happened to my mum with guests waiting patiently at the table, she craftily presented it as 'Cajun Blackened Salmon', which went down extremely well and several guests even requested the recipe)!

Once the salmon is cooked cut it into fillets. Serves eight for a main course or sixteen if chopped smaller for a buffet. Is equally delicious served cold.

SEPTEMBER

Mellow Fruitfullness

Borders' beauty; a history lesson; Riviera of the North; speaking the same language; making the most of soup; swallows' farewell; mushroom breakfasts; fishy tails; luck pennies; a modern Capability Brown; hips and haws and other berries; fruits of autumn; changing colours; preparations for winter begin.

Witchcraft and Wizardry

Northumberland's sweeping hills marked journey's end at Hexham. We – the 'haill unseemly crew' of us, dogs, Doyenne and me – were visiting son Robert and his family in their new home just outside the historic town.

We took the A68, the sunny road which splits Scotland's east Borders between the A7 and the A697. We saw miles and miles of Scotland, looking its best, as Scotland mostly does. The Border hills are bonny hills, deceptively soft-looking compared with our Angus braes, but winter can be as hard and bleak and desolate as anywhere.

Once you've crossed the River Forth and said farewell to Edinburgh head for the high pass of Soutra's summit with the Lammermuir Hills on your left. After Lauder it's onwards south to the Border, with the tops of the Moorfoot Hills marching away westwards. Past Eildon's three peaks, favourite view of Sir Walter Scott and where King Arthur and his Court lie sleeping their enchanted sleep in a great cave entered by a hidden magic doorway. Any mortal stumbling by chance upon the entrance and finding his way into the cave will see before him Arthur's great battle sword and his hunting horn. He must choose between drawing the sword or blowing the horn. Make the right choice and he will become King of all Britain. Make the wrong choice . . . I'll draw a veil over further speculation.

This is not the only legend surrounding these mysterious hills. Sir Thomas of Ercildoune, a true historical figure known as Thomas the Rhymer, met the Queen of Elfland who dazzled his wits and threw a spell over him. She carried him off into the Eildon Hill where she kept him for seven faerie years (which are only as many minutes in the mortal world). She freed him back into the world with the Gift of Truth, which accounts for his other sobriquet of True Thomas.

Michael Scott, the Border Wizard and another real-life knight, played his part in the story of the Eildon Hill which, so it is told, had but one peak originally. The mighty Wizard, finding nothing better to do, one day cleft Eildon into the three peaks we see today, creating the view so beloved of Sir Walter Scott and known as Scott's View.

Close to Earlston is Sorrowlessfield, reputedly so named because it was the only farm in the Borders not to suffer any deaths among its menfolk at the tragic Battle of Flodden in 1513 when Henry VIII's army, commanded by Thomas Howard, Earl of Surrey, devastated the flower of Scotland's fighting men under King James IV. More than 10,000 Scottish soldiers fell that day along with their king and large numbers of the nobility. The awfulness of the defeat was eventually commemorated in the lament 'The Flo'ers o' the Forest'. It is set to words but the tune, played by a solo piper, has been adopted as the final farewell to honour fallen soldiers.

Then Jedburgh with its history of Border reiving and rugby – a difference of pace rather than attitude! Read George MacDonald Fraser's *The Steel Bonnets*, to really appreciate the horrors of the Border reiving years. You'll hear of Jock Half-Lugs Elliot, Nebless Clem Croser and Fingerless Will Nixon. Descriptive bynames or nicknames earned from injuries received in the bloody feuding of these lawless times? Carter Bar is the barren hilltop where you can stand with one foot in England and the other in Scotland. It was indeed a Bar or barrier, the gateway of Scotland. Then it's into Cheviot country, down the long straight

Roman road of Dere Street, across Hadrian's Wall and into Hexham.

Grandson Fergus, who is not yet two, is exhausting. He hasn't learnt to walk yet, he just runs everywhere and you need to keep your eyes peeled or he's into the next calamity. Sheba is very patient with him, seeming to understand that small people are a matter of survival.

Northumberland is a marvellous part of the country to live. Its people and the countryside strongly reflect our own on this side of the border. But I always need back to Angus. Dr Samuel Johnson said, 'the noblest prospect which a Scotchman ever sees, is the high road that leads him to England!' And him with a fine Scots Border name! H.V. Morton's farewell sentiments to Scotland at the end of his inspired travelogue *In Scotland Again*, better reflect my return home. 'Thank you for all the good and kindly things, for friendship, for humour, for beauty.'

Bilingual

Return visits usually mean that previous ones have been a great success. Which is just why the Doyenne and I, and Macbeth too, have spent two restful weeks at Portnockie enjoying a somewhat belated summer holiday. The more we get to know the Banff and Moray coast the more we enjoy returning there. It lived up to its reputation of the 'Riviera of the North' and we had a succession of bright, sunny days. When the rest of the east of Scotland was struggling with the frightful weather of recent weeks, they had twenty-seven days of unbroken sunshine.

I have a passion for harbours and boats thankfully shared, or at least tolerated, by the Doyenne. Without having to go further than Pennan (of film *Local Hero* fame) to the east and Buckie to the west, I was able to indulge my passion. The smaller harbours filling twice a day with the clear, clean ice-blue water of the Moray Firth are no longer the full-time working places of the past. They are mostly filled now with leisure boats and small fishing boats working only part-time for lobsters and crabs. The breakwaters, the enclosing walls built high for protection against the ferocity of the winter seas, tell a story of what a hard, physical life the old fishermen led.

'Sinnine' for Sandend, 'Finechty' for Findochty, 'Gamerie' for Gardenstown – you need a day or two getting acquainted with the local pronunciation of the village names to be sure you are asking the right directions for where you want to go. Ask for bannocks at the baker and you'll be given large, plate-sized pancakes. 'Roweys' are butteries (butter rolls, if you're posh) in Portsoy, but Cathy our neighbour over the fence in Portknockie (there's scarcely eight miles between the two villages), calls them 'rowleys'. They look like flattened breakfast croissants, but because of their high lard content feel greasy to handle. Don't let that put you off – they are from the tradition of north-east baking that grew out of the need for nor-east wives to send their menfolk out to work fired up with energy and protected internally against the harsh weather conditions that sometimes prevail. They are delicious eaten cold but better warmed through, and are certainly not something for the committed dieter. Oatcakes don't present such a problem as they don't appear to have confusing local names. So you can ask for them as such, or just point at them if you're beginning to get flustered and losing your nerve!

The original villages grew up informally around their harbours, unrestricted by the procedural requirements of modern planning laws. Many of the cottages sit gable-end onto the sea, presenting least resistance to the winter gales like boats riding out a storm. Portnockie is the only one to have been built on the cliff top because there was no suitable land by the shore. The twenty or so houses at Crovie ('Crivvie', locally) hang by their eyebrows to the cliff base and are so close to the sea that there's no room for cars, and everything heavy must be conveyed by wheelbarrow.

Inland from this north-facing coast the fields are big, the land is fertile and the harvest had all been cut. It seemed mostly to have been barley, which I suppose is inevitable so close to the distilleries of the

Spey valley, which need the malted barley to start the sublime process of making malt whisky.

Macbeth quite took to village life – folk take a moment to greet you and pass the time of day, and even have a word for a small, white dog. And I was introduced to the Victoria Hotel where we discussed the relative merits of several whiskies which I hadn't met before.

Roadkill

Poor moldywarp, lying quite dead at the side of the road and so easily mistaken for a lump of earth. He seemed to have been hit a glancing blow by a vehicle – quite enough to kill such a small animal – for when Inka brought him to me there was just one drop of blood on his snout.

About fourteen centimetres long (six inches to my generation) from nose to tail tip, and no evidence of fat on his body. The oversized front paws, like shovels compared to the rear ones, still had earth on them as though he had hit the road's foundations and had to surface to cross over. Their subterranean life means you don't often see moles, but what muscular little powerhouses they are. All the power is in their front half and their necks merge into their shoulders, a bit like some athletes you can see on TV. The fur is short, almost velvety in texture, which helps to ease their way through the tunnels they dig in search of worms.

At one time moles were trapped in large numbers and gloves and waistcoats made from the skins. Moleskin fabric was woven to simulate the short, soft, fine fur of its namesake and it developed out of the popularity of the real thing when there was not enough of it to meet demand.

Big Tree Garden

People dream of holidays abroad, and in conversation recently a friend berated our Scottish weather saying he couldn't wait to retire to the south of France, or some other part where the sun shines permanently. We've had family holidays abroad and enjoyed them all, and while I look forward to more trips overseas there is so much of Scotland to revisit and more still to explore. And, anyway, when my time comes I want my bones to rest in my own country.

The Doyenne and I have spent a week's holiday staying with son James and his family at their home near Peebles. The Scottish Borders have been a great favourite since our university days at Edinburgh when we explored them at weekends. Then, when our family were young we regularly took them to a tiny cottage on a farm near Cockburnspath, between Dunbar and Berwick upon Tweed, which we shared with my mother at a rent of £1 per week. What happy days these were, down beside the sea. It was a pretty basic cottage and the rent is unthinkable now.

This most recent holiday we spent a wonderful afternoon at Dawyck (as in Hawick) Garden which is in upper Tweeddale near Stobo, where the Tweed looks more like a large stream than the great river it grows into. Our visit was helped by perfect weather, but we agreed that it was a magical place in any conditions.

Dawyck is one of three gardens which have been left to the care of the Royal Botanic Garden Edinburgh (RBGE) which, along with the RBGE, illustrate the story of Scotland's botanical heritage.

It is predominantly a woodland garden, the result of three hundred years of tree planting to produce one of Scotland's finest arboretums, and it forms a backdrop to the house which is still privately owned. What makes it so special is that, unlike commercially planted woodlands, there is space between the trees to see them as individuals, and to really enjoy their shapes and colours. It's not really the place for dogs, so they stayed behind at the house where they have the freedom of the garden and the certainty of a good walk when we get back.

I've written previously about David Douglas, one of Scotland's famous nineteenth-century plant hunters, and 'father' of the Douglas Fir. An interesting comment was that there would have been fifty per cent fewer specimens of conifer in Dawyck's garden if Douglas had not undertaken his great expeditions. Seeds which he sent back were planted at Dawyck and have grown into some of the tallest trees in Britain.

As we drove away from the garden a travelling farrier was shoeing a horse in a layby. He'd had a puncture, and it was easier for the horse to come to him than for him to get to the horse.

The Next Generation

Silence reigns! It's quite strange. On Monday morning the swallow activity round the house was tremendous – skimming the rooftop and volplaning down to hover briefly and take off again in explosive aerobatics. They dive-bombed the porch at the front door where they've been nesting, twittering and chattering amongst themselves as if saying their farewells for another season. The Doyenne was quite wary of going outside while the aerial dog-fighting was going on. On Tuesday morning all was silent. At some point during the previous day the word was given and the swallows started their long journey to the heat of Africa, leaving us to contemplate the onset of winter. It's astonishing how such a small body can store the energy to travel so many thousands of miles.

Inka fathered four puppies to a sweet yellow bitch

called Ghillie. We took him to see his family before they go off to their new homes – all the way to Dorset for one of them. Three are definitely spoken for, and the wee black bitch may still be looking for an owner. One has already been named Brock and another is being threatened with Snoopy, but I don't think he knows about it yet. (As a footnote to this story the wee black bitch was kept by the breeder and named Maggot. She shows no resentment and I think she's really quite proud of her unconventional title.)

The pups have been a great source of entertainment to the breeder but, like bairns, it's fine to see them leave home! There was a narrow squeak with one of them which disappeared down a rabbit hole on a personal expedition of exploration. They are all still so roly-poly that once he was down there he might not have been able to wriggle back out again.

A most unusual sight has greeted the breeder in recent mornings. She's found mallard ducks, very much alive although missing several feathers, sitting in the kennel along with the puppies. There's a pond nearby and the only explanation that has been offered so far is that the mother dog must have gone out each night and picked up an unsuspecting duck roosting by the pond side.

Was it just the inbred Labrador instinct to retrieve? Or the mother's way of telling her pups that it's time to face a cruel world and showing them what food alternatives are available once the milk supply dries up? Whatever the reason there are some mighty relieved ducks flying around telling a story that none of the other ducks believe.

Dog Walking

Two fields at the back of the house, which had been in 'set-aside', have now been ploughed and sown. 'Set-aside' means they were taken out of production and left uncropped for this past season. Being uncultivated meant they looked a bit scruffy but, agricultural policies aside, there were definite benefits for a man with two dogs to walk every day.

Inka could clear the garden fence with one bound, but Macbeth had to be lifted over as it is rabbit-proofed with chicken wire along its length – so it's Macbeth-proof too. In the absence of the usual agricultural management the weeds grew freely providing cover for the nesting oystercatchers and meadow pipits which I have mentioned in past articles.

The stream, which flows along the bottom of the garden, separates the two fields. Pheasants and mallards nested along its banks. Several pairs of partridge produced families in the long grass at the foot of the beech hedges. And there will have been plenty more activity which I missed.

It was great to have such a good walk just outside the back door, but nothing stays the same forever. With the combine harvesting all finished there are stubble fields aplenty for us to walk in until the agricultural round gets up to speed once again and they too will be ploughed, ready to be sown with next year's crops.

We – the dogs and I, that is – sat down for a breather on the embankment of the long-abandoned Brechin to Edzell railway line. Little reports all around me, sounding like a distant battle, caught my attention. It was the dried seed pods on the whins bursting with the heat of the sun and spraying their seeds into the undergrowth – their method of regeneration. I counted twelve seeds in one pod. Most of the seeds will be eagerly eaten by birds but some will remain unnoticed to germinate and produce new bushes. It's not just popular breakfast cereals that go 'Snap, Crackle, Pop'.

Fat Boy's Breakfast

Wild mushrooms picked, first thing, from the field beside the house, gently fried in butter while the dogs are being fed, and eaten for breakfast with grilled bacon and grilled tomatoes, has got to be one of life's more wanton pleasures.

Field mushrooms have darker gills on the underside than the shop variety, and a more distinct taste. Tossing them into the frying pan with the dew still on them is another of nature's rewards for living in the country. Words aren't enough; you have to hear the sizzle and smell the faintly earthy aroma to truly appreciate the pleasure.

The local, home-grown tomatoes which we buy just now from the Trinity (Taranty, locally) Garden Centre, just outside Brechin, taste and look different too. Like my father, I love tomatoes – the taste of them and the texture of them. Half a century ago their season was restricted to just a few weeks in the year. Now, 'airmiles' tomatoes are flown in from all round the world and we can buy them off the supermarket shelves all year. The Taranty tomatoes have a heady, tangy flavour that dominates your taste buds – perhaps being grown, harvested and eaten in their proper season helps.

Fifty years ago and more, during the school holidays, I used to cycle across to visit Jim Tindal who leased the walled garden of Usan House, near Ferryden, as a market garden. I can remember vividly, in the summer time, being allowed to eat – warm off the vine – the undersized tomatoes which couldn't be sold. Today they call them cherry tomatoes, and market them as something special. They were something special then, it was just that nobody had thought of marketing them as such.

There was also an old fig tree trained along the wall of the glasshouse. It had been producing sweet, juicy figs for decades and I picked them and ate them straight from the branch. Ripe, warm figs and baby tomatoes

– there are few things to compare with these sun-burst childhood memories.

Making Do

An ingin intil't, a courgette intil't, two leeks, several sticks of celery and a vegetable stock cube all went intil't. I'm sure it was my favourite travel writer, H. V. Morton, who wrote similarly about the making of a pot of broth which had scraps of beef from the Sunday joint, a handful of barley, salt and all manner of vegetables thrown into it or 'intil't'. The resulting feast of a meal was served up and put before him for his dinner.

We were home after a weekend visit to son James and his family in the Borders and the Doyenne was keen to leave me some soup for my own lunch the following day. There was little in the vegetable rack or the fridge but, like the true thrifty Yorkshire girl she is, she made the best of what was to hand. I'm sure I lunched as well as did old H. V. – and I have the silhouette to prove it.

It was buying a couple of finnan haddies that set off this train of thought. Caroline on the fish van from Gourdon said folk hardly ask for this once-popular smoked fish delicacy. Originating in the fishing village of Findon, just south of Aberdeen, they are whole haddocks split and left on the bone, salted and lightly smoked. Not to be confused with ordinary smoked haddock which has been filleted off the bone, nor with an Arbroath smokie, which is much more heavily smoked, as is obvious from its burnished golden tobacco colour.

A finnan haddie isn't a difficult meal to prepare, even I can do it – just poach it in milk, or half milk and half water. The uncooked fish has a translucent look to it and it should be poached until the flesh turns opaque. For extra deliciousness add a poached or scrambled egg and, if you like the idea, some spinach on the side.

Finnan haddie is the fishy ingredient of Cullen Skink, that most traditional east coast of Scotland soup and, flaked off the bone after poaching, it goes well in kedgeree. My mother used to say that they were smoking haddies in Findon long before the fisherfolk of Auchmithie started to smoke what ultimately became the Arbroath Smokie!

Scots cooks and Yorkshire cooks have long traditions of thrift and resourcefulness. The Doyenne has told me that in centuries past the Yorkshire pudding was put on the table and eaten first, and the joint of beef held back in case marauding Scots came by and stole the meat. While I'm all for marauding Scots I'm not sure I go for her explanation, as the marauding Scots had a habit of coming back the way they went, mopping up what they'd missed.

As for thrift, what can beat the haggis, the culmination of Scottish gastronomic versatility? Oatmeal, suet and the liver, heart and lights (lungs) of a sheep, a large ingin (onion) sliced small, seasoned well and all sewn up in a sheep's stomach. A prime example of waste not, want not, as my father used to ding into me and my sister.

Now, if folk don't ask for finnan haddies sooner or later they'll stop smoking them, and then we'll all say how much we miss them. I know I would.

I Ken Mysel' by the Queer-like Smell that the Next Stop's Kirkcaddy.

A journey by train to Edinburgh always takes me back to when I was a youngster, waving goodbye to my parents standing on the station platform, as the old steam train pulled out for the journey from Montrose to Musselburgh, and the start of a new term at boarding school. There have been changes to the towns and the countryside along the way of the railway line, but the landscape remains unchanged from how it was over fifty years ago. The two great railway bridges over Tay and Forth, monuments to the best traditions of Scottish engineering, are both showing signs of their age now, but they've stayed in better shape for a lot longer than their road-bridge counterparts.

Fife didn't call itself a county but rather styled itself the Kingdom of Fife – it probably still does. James VI of Scotland described Fife's weather-sculpted coastline as, 'A beggar's mantle fringed with gold.' He was referring to that string of gems, then-important ports which traded with their Hanseatic counterparts, which have evolved into today's fishing villages of Crail, Cellardyke, Anstruther (Enster, locally), Pittenweem, St Monans and Lower Largo where, coincidentally, Robinson Crusoe came from. It was an apt description then and has lost none of its redolence over the centuries.

The three peaks of the Lomond Hills, seen to the west of the railway, are the highest points in this richly ag-ricultural county. Meaning 'beacon hills', there are the remains of a Pictish fort on one peak. It was an obvious place to put a beacon to warn others of approaching danger.

Once past Kirkcaldy, the line runs alongside the shore, and looking east and down the Firth of Forth you can see the old volcanic plug of North Berwick Law, free-standing like the Lomond Hills in a flat agricultur-al plain. On Saturdays we used to cycle down the coast from school in Musselburgh and climb the Law for the view. There was an arch made from a whale's jawbones on the summit, but I'm told that it finally collapsed from old age some years ago. During the Napoleonic Wars a signalling station was built on the hilltop – the highest conspicuous point for warning the populace of a French invasion.

Throwing a coin from the carriage window as the train crossed the Forth Bridge was supposed to bring good luck. Us penny-wise schoolboys always had a half-penny in our sporrans to inspire good fortune over the coming weeks. Today's train windows are sealed shut, so the coins stay in the pooch and good luck whistles in the wind.

As the train nears the Forth Bridge, and looking south over the water, the old extinct volcano of Arthur's Seat guards Edinburgh, scene of my student days and where the Doyenne and I met (Edinburgh University, of course, not Arthur's Seat). The military and defensive value of a hilltop was made good use of here too, for evidence of an Iron-Age fort has been found. And there's been a fortress on Edinburgh's Castle Rock, another extinct volcano, for more than thirty centuries. 'I to the hills will lift mine eyes', wrote the psalmist. I always will.

As an aside, we had a neighbour called Arthur Budge with whom I used to drink gin and tonic! One of our sons, still at primary school, was explaining to us what he had learnt at school about Arthur's Seat or 'You know,' he said, 'Mr Budge's Chair!'

Life in the Country

Agricultural roups, or auction sales, take place outdoors

in all weathers and they attract a hardier breed of participant than the usual urban emporiums of un-fulfilled temptation and impulse buying.

Mearns Vintage Vehicle Club's Annual Rally, held last weekend at Arnhall Farm, near Edzell, started its festivities on Saturday with a roup of diverse vintage vehicle spare parts, ailing machinery and implements and a selection of second-hand equipment. An eclectic mix of ancient and modern you might say – pretty much how you could describe the followers of the event!

The auctioneer had the traditional six-shooter patter of his calling. He obviously knew his audience and he played them like a well-tuned fiddle. He could be heard encouraging assorted Alecs and Willies to reach deeper into their pooches (trouser pockets) and part with that extra pound that would capture the prize of the day.

I suspect that some lots, bought in a frenzy of denial to other bidders, remained hidden beneath sacks in the boot of the car, to be surreptitiously removed under cover of darkness to a dusty corner of their new owners' outbuildings. Then, unearthed in a year's time to cries of, 'Mercy, so that's where that got to. It'll maybe fetch a bob or two at the roup.' It's a harmless conveyor belt of endless recycling, which continues with the approval of indulgent wives who see it as a way of keeping their husbands out of worse trouble.

One man was taking a note of every price 'on the hammer', as they call it when the hammer falls and

each lot was sold. He didn't say what he was going to do with his wee notebook and all its figures, but he's probably got an indulgent wife too. Somebody said the auctioneer wasn't an auctioneer at all, but a jeweller from Mintlaw, in Aberdeenshire. It shows how I was so spellbound by the whole atmosphere that I accepted this information without so much as batting an eye.

A notice at the field gate announced that entry was £1 – 'no ifs, no buts.' The lady taking the money looked pretty stern so I handed over the cash without a murmur. Another notice instructed that dogs must be kept on leads at all times, which would have been an affront to Macbeth's and Inka's spirit of independence. It was as well that they'd been left at home.

There is a serious side to the Club members' activities. Each year they raise money for charitable causes, so the more support they get for their weekend festival the more these needy causes benefit. This two-day annual event provides insights into rural life, so town folk leading sheltered 'toonser' lives should make a note to come along to it next year. I'll be there on the Sunday to write about the rally of vintage tractors, static engines, motor cycles, cars and all the rest of the excitement.

Poisonous

Capability Brown was the eighteenth century's greatest English landscape architect. The gardens at Alnwick

Castle, in Northumberland, were first laid out by locally-born Brown in 1750, and remained one of the grandest extravaganzas of that county until the start of the twentieth century.

After a century's decline, in 2000 the present Duchess of Northumberland had a vision of a new garden and, using the historic footprint of previous gardens, started the monumental task of creating the twenty-first century's response to Capability Brown. The Doyenne had several times talked about visiting the gardens and last weekend we made the trip.

I had some misgivings as we entered the very modern visitor centre and pavilion but the moment we were in the garden proper all my doubts vanished. The old landscaped parklands, which had been derelict and forgotten, have been transformed. We were bowled over by the visual interest and sheer exuberance of the flowers, foliage and planting patterns which have been achieved in just eight years. Sadly, the anticipated romantic and fragrant experience of the Rose Garden was marred by the shocking wet weather of the previous weeks.

Eight mirror-polished stainless steel water sculptures are concealed within the topiary coils of the Serpent Garden, illustrating different aspects of water and how it can be made to move. Alongside is the Bamboo Labyrinth which rustles conspiratorially in response to even the lightest breeze.

Belladonna and rhubarb leaves are two of the potentially fatal plants in The Poison Garden, and the Doyenne's insistence that she wanted to visit this feature sent a wee, cold shiver down my spine! 'These Plants Can Kill' announces the notice on the locked gates, and entry to the garden is only under supervision of trained Poison Garden Wardens.

The original walled garden has been laid out as the Ornamental Garden with 16,500 plants to produce colour and scent throughout the year. The slightly absurd memory that stands out of a quite intoxicating experience, is the crab apple trees laden with fruit hanging like bunches of grapes. There's too much to take in at once, and we've already made up our minds that we'll be returning to Alnwick next year.

Surprisingly, for all the vegetation and wildlife-friendly cover, we hardly saw any songbirds. A small colony of peacock butterflies on white buddleia and several species of bees feeding on bugbane was all the insect life to be seen.

We were neither of us greatly impressed by The Grand Cascade, a series of waterfalls obviously intended to be the focal point of the entire garden. I'm sure it's a matter of waiting till it beds down properly into its natural setting for it to properly re-enact the splendour of previous centuries. The Alnwick Garden has a long way to go and there are ambitious plans for further development.

Flying a Kite

My gardening skills are mostly confined to cutting the grass and thereafter admiring the labour and skills of my betters. Now is the time of year when I look forward to putting away the lawnmower, and putting my feet up until springtime. Sadly it never works out that way. The autumn equinox passed on the twenty-second of this month, marking the start of autumn proper when the trees begin to shed their leaves, and it's back to the tedious task of sweeping them up.

A neighbour has found a novel way to use the leaves which gather in the corners of his garden, and produce an interesting planter for bulbs and flowers. Recycling an old, square recycling bin he formed an envelope of chicken wire all round it and about one third of the way down on the inside. He stuffed the envelope with dry beech leaves to a thickness of four or five inches and filled the tub with earth. The finished product is economical and practical, and has a pleasing, rustic look.

I was warned to keep the dogs away from a particular part of the woods because a hare doe had been seen with two newly-born leverets. This seemed unusually late for hares to be breeding and I did some research on the internet. Clicking onto the Loch Leven National Nature Reserve website I found, to my surprise, that their breeding season lasts from March to September, and that a doe can produce up to three litters a year.

I then got reports of swallows producing a third clutch of eggs, and woodpeckers hatching a second brood of chicks. I called on my old friend Alasdair Tindal's near-encyclopaedic knowledge of birds. He confirmed that while it is not common, it is not unusual for swallows to produce three broods, but he had always regarded woodpeckers as single-brood birds.

He went on to tell me about the buzzard he watched recently, circling above his house. It took several minutes for the penny to drop. From the deeply forked tail and effortless, soaring flight with scarcely a beat of the long, slender wings, he was in fact watching a kite. Now, I think that is most unusual for this part of north-east Scotland.

I always appreciate feedback from these weekly pieces. A phone call from Jack Drummond followed the mention last week of Capability Brown. Like the great gardener, Jack is Northumbrian by birth, but he became a Montrosian by adoption having been posted to Montrose Aerodrome as a young man in 1937 after joining the RAF.

Jack told me that on his mother's side he is a direct descendant of Capability Brown. I wondered if Jack had been born with 'green fingers' too, but it turns out that, like me, he's really a fair weather gardener. Well, someone needs to stand back and applaud!

From the Doyenne's Kitchen

HOME GROWN BREAKFAST

This isn't really a recipe, it's just the most satisfying collection of locally sourced goodies.

Our daughters-in-law both keep hens and when they visit they bring gifts of eggs. We have regular Farmers' Markets in both Montrose and Forfar where I buy bacon at the Fife-based Puddledub Pork stall. Our local butcher makes her own black pudding. I buy homegrown tomatoes from the Trinity Garden Centre – the Man with Two Dogs eats them like sweeties, but he can be forgiven for that when he comes in from a walk with a large handkerchief or a cap full of chanterelles.

Bacon, eggs, black pudding, tomato and chanterelles. There can't be a better breakfast!

Not wanting to be left out, son James suggests a good post-party breakfast to clear the head.

BACON AND EGG PITTAS

4 slices of smoked bacon
8 eggs beaten
6 wholemeal pittas
olive oil
butter

Method

Cut the bacon into little squares and fry in the oil in a large frying pan. Add the eggs until nicely scrambled and season to taste. Toast and butter the pitta breads and fill with the mixture for a fuss- and mess-free party-recovery breakfast!

OCTOBER

Hounds of Heaven

Salmon and water kelpies; the hounds of heaven; more about geese; good manners; flying fish and a wee dram; glen soup; conkers; a singular lady; child labour; death of a dog; look out for fairy rings on the lawn and beefsteak fungi on old trees.

Floral Tribute

Salmon leaping up the turbulent waters of the River North Esk was the highlight of last week. I've seen the river level a lot higher when the force of water prevented the salmon from moving upriver, but they made good progress in the hour or so that we sat watching them.

It was the enduring struggle – an eternal one – of these wild fish to return to the fresh headwaters of their mother stream to spawn and produce future generations of the 'king of fish'.

Macbeth and I had walked down the river, past the Rocks of Solitude, and sat on a rocky outcrop watching the peaty brown water. If you take a scramble off the track by the riverside and peer down from some of the high cliffy overhangs, they hide some black, silent pools.

It doesn't take much to stir the imagination. Cold, sinister, fathomless and home to who knows what kelpies and other water spirits. But there must be some kindly ones among them which ensure that the salmon continue their instinctive migration to the spawning beds, or 'redds' as they are technically known.

As the fish struggled through the rushing current I watched some of them nosing into the calmer water of the salmon ladder in their urgency to continue their progress upstream. Compared with fish ladders on other rivers, such as the one on the River Tummel at Pitlochry, this is very simple. Just a series of steps cut through the riverbank rock to form an easier passage for the fish.

None seemed to need to rely on the ladder, and in the urge to get home they leapt into the heart of the cascade and disappeared on the next stage of their journey. There were some handsome fish of twelve and fifteen pounds, but even grilse of five or six pounds were undeterred. It was a special hour because you can't arrange an experience like that to order. The constant commotion of the water clears the mind of daily clutter. By the time we were ready to walk back up the river to the car I was ready to tilt at windmills!

As we rounded a corner on the walk back to the car we surprised a red squirrel which shot up a nearby tree leaning precariously out over the river. Higher and higher it climbed, balancing with its brush-like tail, and with its long claws perfectly adapted to its tree-dwelling lifestyle there was no fear of it losing its grip and falling into the water.

A bunch of red carnations had been left by the river-side on the rocks at The Loups. Someone's poignant memory being revisited? No one seems to know.

Hounds of Heaven

I popped into the barbers for my usual session with Dennis Burke who has cut the greying locks for more years than either of us care to admit.

Dennis told me that driving into Montrose that morning to open the shop he had seen more pink-footed geese roosting on the mudflats of Montrose Basin than he could remember for a long time. After he had smartened me up I went round to Montrose Station where I knew I could get a tremendous clear view over the Basin from the passenger footbridge that crosses the railway lines, away over the water and onto the hills beyond.

The tidal estuary which is the Basin is an internationally important wetland for migratory birds and waders, ducks and geese. I grew up thinking it was just an enormous mudflat that appeared twice a day at low tide. Its importance began to be understood after the late Sir Peter Scott, the naturalist and conservationist, came to Montrose in the 1950s and did a radio programme about the diversity of wildfowl the Basin held. It now belongs to, and is managed by, the Scottish Wildlife Trust as a wildlife reserve.

On the approach to Montrose Station the embankment carrying the railway line runs alongside the Basin's high-water mark. Passengers looking westwards out of their compartment windows, or like me from the elevation of the passenger bridge, towards the Grampian Mountains are always assured of memorable views whatever the state of the tide. I know of no other railway station which commands such a panoramic backdrop.

The incoming tide was pushing the birds onto the mud-banks. Their wild cries blew across on the wind, and I thought about the clocks going back soon, and the mornings darkening again as winter begins to set in. Packs of geese took off with choruses of farewells to those who lingered on, and headed to all points of the compass in search of feeding grounds. They are not welcomed by farmers when they descend to graze on the fields of winter barley whose first green shoots are beginning to push through. They pull the shoots out by the roots leaving the plant no chance of recovery, and their large webbed feet paddle the ground into a hard pan which restricts the crop's growth and costs the farmer money.

Mallard and eider duck were wading in the shallows at the back of the station platform, and a delicate wisp of dunlins flittered along the tideline. Two oyster-catchers pattered over the oozy mud, busily poking with their orange beaks for oozy mud treats which I imagine are their equivalent of dark chocolate.

I'm reading a most entertaining book called *The Longshoreman* by Richard Shelton, who calls the geese, 'hounds of heaven'. Out with the dogs for their last-thing-at-night walk when the frost is iron hard, and hearing the distant yelps of the geese closing in on you, it's easy to imagine them as baying hounds in hot pursuit.

I met one of my primary school teachers who told me she enjoys reading these Saturday pieces. I told her how much I enjoy writing them, and we got to wondering if her efforts all those years ago had contributed to the quality of the words. We agreed they probably had. I don't remember the same easy rapport between us when I was eight years old!

Scottish Fall

Doom-laden predictions of dreadful weather, from the weather girls to the editor of a prominent Dundee publication, greeted the announcement that we – the Doyenne and I, and Macbeth too – were off to the west coast for a week's holiday.

As we dropped down the hill to Loch Melfort we were dazzled by the brilliance of the sunset and smiled to ourselves, thinking, 'red sky at night, Whitsons' delight'. However, I hadn't taken account of the long reach of editorial influence. The following morning the heavens opened and chastised us for our presumption. It rained every day but, in fairness, there were welcome breaks in the weather when we got out for walks and drives in the car.

It's the time of the Scottish 'fall' and the leaves on the trees are changing to their autumn colours. Hot reds, yellows, ochre and every shade of brown change the palette of the landscape. The crotal brown of dead bracken was everywhere and the burns were foaming full with the colour of dark beer.

We had a memorable drive on the little B road from Kilmelfort to Dalavich over a real switchback of a track on which every serious gradient is marked 1:6. One glorious view follows another and in the ten miles to Dalavich we met only one car. As we drove along Loch Awe back to Taynuilt and the coast, we saw the tops of Ben Cruachan and the neighbouring mountains covered in snow. When we stopped for a walk to the Avich Falls there had been endless new smells to delight a small, white dog.

Poetry in Nature

The geese are back – it's more than a fortnight since I saw the first of them down in the Lothians. But one skein passing over the house earlier this week particularly caught my attention.

They were beating down from the north, heading Montrose Basin way, and there was a steadfastness about their flight that made me think they must have just flown in from Spitzbergen, or some other far-flung arctic cape. It was the final leg of an annual journey that's been replayed over generations, and the birds would be anticipating the relief from the exertion and exhaustion of so many hundreds of miles of relentless flight. Driven by compulsive instinct, nothing could divert them from their intuitive flight path. They would shortly touch down for a 'wash and brush-up' on the muddy banks of Montrose Basin before moving out to stubble fields to graze.

'And aye their cryin' voices trailed ahint them on the air,' wrote Violet Jacob in her poem 'The Wild Geese' from her *Songs of Angus* first published in 1915. Regular readers of my column know that Violet Jacob is one of my literary heroes who, despite her aristocratic up-bringing, wrote so naturally in the authentic Angus vernacular that she learnt first-hand as a child from her daily contact with countryside folk.

I attended a conference at the Burn House at Edzell.

Built in 1791, it's a fine example of a Georgian mansion cleverly sited, as so many grand houses of that period were, to sit sympathetically within its surroundings. They had great enthusiasm then for planting trees, and the ability and vision to see in their mind's eye the mature trees occupying their place in the landscape and in relation to each other. I mentioned this to one of the other delegates and I liked her answer: 'They knew what it meant to lift the soul just by looking at nature.'

Minding My Ps and Qs

I'd had reason to give Sheba the most awful rollicking for some misdemeanour or other. A few moments later I bent down and she took the opportunity to nip my behind. The message was clear – mind my manners when there's a lady about!

Flying Fish

Holiday cottages and family pets don't always go together, but the Doyenne and I have come back from a week's holiday at Loch Melfort where dogs are welcome.

We stayed in a cottage at the time-share complex at

Melfort Village, sixteen miles below Oban. It's the sort of place where it's very easy to give into temptation to eat more and exercise less. Having the dogs with us meant we got out amongst the marvellous west-coast scenery which we enjoy so much. And the autumn colours of the trees and landscape are quite spectacular at this time of year. Grandchildren are welcome too, and Alfie and Mathilda, plus parents, joined us for half the week. The swimming pool within the complex was a great hit with the youngsters, and there are play areas and lots of other activities.

We found a wonderful fishmonger in Tarbert Loch Fyne where we got the freshest scallops and sea bass. The scallops, wrapped in streaky bacon and grilled, are still a melt-in-the-mouth memory. The Doyenne baked the sea bass, stuffing them with breadcrumbs and parsley bound together with lemon juice. Speechless!

The 'Shower of Herring' restaurant is part of the Melfort complex, and is named after a real shower of herring which rained out of the sky in 1821. This is one of a number of similarly documented biblical-style phenomena. It's thought the fish got caught up some sort of a waterspout which ran out of energy when it got over land and deposited its unlikely passengers.

You meet all sorts at a place like Melfort. We met a man from Buchlyvie which is a very well-to-do village on the road from Stirling to Loch Lomond. Here's the sort of story they tell in Buchlyvie. A man was handed a glass of his host's favourite malt whisky. He looked at the liquid scarcely covering the bottom of the glass, held it to the light, sniffed it, and asked its age. 'Fifteen years old,' his host replied proudly. 'It's very small for its age,' was the comment!

The Living Glen

The dogs and I made a swift executive decision and took ourselves up Glen Esk to blow away the cobwebs and enjoy a bit of space. Walks have to take account of Inka's long legs and Macbeth's sawn-off short ones. I spend my time with one eye on Inka to make sure he's not bounding out of sight, and turning back to urge Macbeth to get a shift on!

It was warm and sunny – a perfect autumn day. The mood and character of the hills changed continually as the shadows of the clouds were chased across the brae faces. The bloom is off the heather and the bracken has died away to its winter crotal brown, but the browns, greens and grey of the rocks and scree take on new life when the sun breaks through the clouds again. All up the glen there's still a terrific showing of ripe rowans – 'the sentinel rowan's scarlet flame' – as Montrose poet, Helen B. Cruickshank, wrote.

A handsome carving of an osprey, carrying a large trout in its talon, has been erected by the side of the road at Migvie. This is a farm in the glen called Migvie, not to be confused with the village and church of the same name in Aberdeenshire that I wrote of earlier, and it marks the south-eastern boundary of the Cairngorm National Park. A ready availability of food in Loch Lee has attracted these birds to the district. If you are lucky, you can see one sweeping down to the water and scooping out an unsuspecting fish for tea.

I stopped to have a peer over the bridge at Dalbrack. After the terrific rains last weekend the water was still dark and peaty, like Newcastle Brown Ale, broken with white rapids and fairly scooring through the narrow gorge beneath the bridge. The rise in water level will help the autumn run of salmon to make it to the head-waters and the spawning redds.

Afterwards we walked up to the Scottish Water filtration plant at Whitehillocks. As we drove away we met half a dozen garrons and a foal, straggled across the road at the foot of Glen Effock. The shaggy-maned ponies are used to carry the deer off the hill after they have been shot. As they sniffed inquisitively around the car a confident cock pheasant strolled unconcern-edly around their legs, making his way to only he knew where.

The rejuvenated Retreat Folk Museum has one of the best records of the history of the glen as well as an ex-tensive genealogical database. After renovations and the completion of an extension to the building the mu-seum has now got most of its exhibits back on show for visitors. It is well worth a visit to learn more about country life in past centuries, especially in the glen it-self. It also has an excellent restaurant, so we stopped for a piping bowl of spicy carrot soup which calmed the raging pangs of hunger. There's an awful lot to see and do, and think about, up a glen.

Worse than the Curate's Egg

The mysteries of nature continue to confound me. Out with the dogs for their morning walk I found an olive-green egg lying in the pathway. It couldn't have been there long because it's a busy path and it would soon have been trodden on by man or dog.

I took it home and put it in a safe corner of the kitchen while I saw the Doyenne off to her office. While I dealt with the mail I became increasingly aware of quite one of the most offensive smells I can remember. It was so bad I began to wonder if La D. had been careless about what she was putting down the sink, or perhaps a dog had forgotten his manners! It didn't take too much longer to realise that it was the egg which was the cause of my discomfort.

I took the offending object outside and cut it open. The yolk had decomposed into a black sludge and the smell was even worse, if that was possible. So I threw it into the stream. What I cannot understand is why a six-month-old egg should have been transferred so carefully to the ground, rather than hurled out of the nest with the least possible ceremony.

Last weekend was hectic with grandchildren. Both sons visited with their families, and the Doyenne and I were on the go full tilt. One of the highlights of his visit was grandson Alfie finally getting to terms with riding a bike. It fair warmed my heart to see his father peching up and down the drive as Alfie mastered balancing on two wheels, and at the same time pedalling and pointing the bike in a straight line. It took me back to when I did the same for Alfie's dad.

Another high point was collecting conkers while we were out with the dogs. The youngsters seemed to have just as much enthusiasm for conkers that I remember when I was their age. Whenever two-year-old granddaughter Mathilda found one she was so excited she might have found a rare and precious jewel. We also found sweet chestnuts encased in their prickly hedgehog-like shells. The nuts aren't big enough for human consumption this year, but the squirrels and wood pigeons are greedily devouring them.

I had my first game of curling of the new season. For some reason I recalled an independent-minded lady member of our club who curled for many years very much by her own rules. When you throw a curling stone you are meant to aim for the (sweeping) broom held by your skip (team captain) at the far end of the ice rink, who 'gives you the ice' to aim for. If he is clever the skip will have anticipated the action of the stone as it 'curls' up the ice. The player who 'lays' (throws) the stone must endeavour to throw it with the right weight and impetus to reach the red, white and blue circles, or 'house', at the far end. If they both get it right the stone will finish at the other end of the rink, at precisely the spot where the skip wishes it.

Whenever this lady member was upbraided by her

skip for not 'playing to the broom', she would comment to the rest of the rink (team): 'I dinna bather wi' him. I aye just taks my ain ice!' (I don't bother about him. I always choose my own ice).

Acquiring the Work Ethic

The grandchildren's arrival to spend a night with us set me thinking about the tattie holidays which used to be the reason for children having a fortnight off school at this time of year. Before the days of mechanical harvesters farmers could never have lifted their crop before the winter set in without the squads of youngsters and adults bent double lifting the potatoes by hand. Some families depended on the extra income to buy winter clothes and other essentials. Everyone got a 'bit', or length of a potato drill (or 'dreel') to pick, and the little ones got a half bit which meant half pay, and wasn't good news!

Potatoes were mostly lifted by hand when our own children were growing up and once they were old enough they set out each morning to the neighbouring farms with their midday piece in their piecey bag. It was an opportunity to earn better money than they would have done at home, and the money was theirs to spend how they wished. It was hard work and they soon learned that getting roared at by the farm grieve, and chased to work harder, was how life was. But one thing's for sure – it helped them understand the work ethic, which they all still have.

The dogs and I were walking round a wee lochan when Inka disturbed a waterhen at the bank. It's been an age since I've seen one and I'm wondering if there are fewer about or whether I've just not been in the right places at the right time. When we lived at Logie Pert there was always a pair or two roosting or nesting along the side of the Gallery Burn which ran through the garden, and I would waken sometimes in the night with their calls, 'kurruk, kurruk', which are surprisingly loud and deep for such a small bird.

Their flight is weak and they fly low over the water, trailing their legs so that their feet patter over the surface. Above my desk I have a print of a waterhen taking flight, which was done by my predecessor Colin Gibson. He wrote this column for over forty years and embellished each week's article with a black and white scraperboard drawing, and my print illustrates his own story about waterhens.

Sometimes the smallest things can illuminate my day. I picked up a feather about three inches long from the grass beside the bird table at the back door. It's mostly light grey or fawn in colour, but what caught my attention was the narrow, vivid yellow stripe along the top of it. It's been sitting on the corner of the desk for the last four days and it's only now that the colour is beginning to fade. I'm trying to identify its owner and I think from the yellow flash that it must be a secondary feather from a greenfinch's wing.

Death of a Friend

Conkers, geese, waking up to frost on the car windows in the mornings – all autumn's awaited calling cards. I remember at prep school, the excitement and competition to be first to grab the conkers that fell from the big chestnut tree. At the end of each class there was an unseemly scramble to get out of the classroom and round to the tree to see if any more of the shiny nuts had fallen.

I never weary of writing about the geese. Out first thing with the dogs I watched a skein of them flying north, framed by the morning sun against a cloudless blue sky. The steady beating chevron was so high they must have been aiming to clear the Cairn o' Mount for a destination somewhere about Aboyne in Deeside. Later, out for the main walk, the afternoon sun caught the tiny silver shape of an airliner flying westwards many times higher than the geese – on its way to America, no doubt.

It's just needed a couple of the frosty nights to kill off a lot of the mushrooms and fungi that littered the woods and fields. What's left are blackening, decomposing ex-crescences in their death throes, some of which were very colourful a fortnight ago, although some were fair-ly repulsive in the first place. But there are still flashes of colour, if you keep your eyes open. I've found three clusters of bright saffron-orange yellow stagshorn fun-gus growing in the rotting stumps of old conifers.

There's much talk, and increasing television coverage, of the rewards from gathering nature's wild bounty, eat-ing off the land and eating for free. Regular readers will know that we heartily endorse the idea in this house-hold. We practised what we preach last weekend when we were lucky enough to be given a haunch of roe deer venison.

The Doyenne marinated it for two days in olive oil, celery, onion, juniper berries, orange rind, our own parsley and thyme, seasoning and red wine. Slow roast-ed on a bed of root vegetables, the gravy was made from the juices from the roast and the liquidised vegetables, and flavoured with her own redcurrant jelly. Served up with the Doyenne's home-made rowan and apple jelly (made last September), the meat was pink and moist and tender – and our guests seemed to approve.

Pudding was the Doyenne's bramble and apple pie and a bramble mousse.

The apples were a gift and I'd picked four and a half pounds of brambles from the roadsides close to home (I'm still picking the thorns out of my fingers).

So there's a call now for more brambles to go into the freezer for the Christmas pies, or else there will be uproar from the family when they come to visit.

I'm sad to report that Inka, our black Labrador, is dead. It would have been less of a blow if he had been an elderly dog, but he was only four years old, so his death was unexpected. He was bred close to where we live and much of his life he ran about woods and fields which were home territory. And how he loved to run. He could have galloped round seven parishes and scarcely drawn breath. The only time I gave him free rein was on the beach where he was always in view, and he loved that freedom.

The sea, indeed water generally, was a huge attraction but then Labradors are traditionally water dogs, so he was a natural and strong swimmer. He had a daft habit of pushing his whole muzzle underwater trying to pick large stones off the sea or the river bed, and I always got so impatient with him.

Remarks that he was a 'super, joyful character' and a 'lovely character' sum him up very well. He was an extrovert, genial dog who took it for granted that everyone he met shared his joy for living. Bounding up to greet other walkers it was occasionally clear that his infectious enthusiasm was not always immediately shared. Sometimes he had to be reintroduced once calm had been restored.

If he could have had his way he'd have had me out walking all day every day. I used to try and pull on my

233

boots without him realising, but however secretively I did so, a sixth sense told him what I was up to and he'd be capering around in front of me panting with excitement and urging me to 'get a shift on!' because there were smells to smell and places to explore.

Macbeth misses his chum. Although very much the smaller of the two, he was undisputed leader in the house. In the early days, Inka naively imagined that both bowls of food were meant for him. Without any intervention from us Macbeth sorted out the problem, and his food could lie untouched by black dogs for a whole day until he was ready to eat it.

Outdoors, with his longer legs, Inka tended to go his own way. But the two of them had a game that never ceased to entertain us. Inka would gallop as fast as he could in circles round Macbeth. He had the speed but Macbeth had manoeuvrability and would judge the moment to cut across Inka's bows, barking and snapping at his legs. I wish we could have recorded it because both dogs so clearly enjoyed the fun.

It's just as well Macbeth seems to be made of old boots, even if they are rather small ones, because Inka's death has left a bigger hole in our lives than we might have expected.

The deaths of both Sheba and Inka brought many kind letters and cards all of which the Doyenne and I greatly appreciated. An e-mail from Kansas, sent to the Dundee *Courier* following Inka's death, was forwarded to me by the paper:

> If you would, pass on this note of appreciation and con-dolence to Angus who writes the Man With Two Dogs column. Thank you.
>
> Dear Angus and the rest of the family: I was sorry to read about the loss of Inka. I hope you get another dog when you are ready. I have been reading your columns on the web for nearly two years, since our male Westie, Jasper, died at seventeen. While mourning him and hunting for a new puppy, I came upon your columns. I read back through the entire archive and keep up weekly. Your stories lifted my heart out of its sadness and connected me with more tales like the ones my grand-mother Margie Munro used to tell me of our ancestors' home in the Highlands. I have shared your stories with many Westie breeders and show people all over the US. When we got our new puppy, Rufus, I started him on a daily hour-long walk in the woods near our home in Kansas. Your tales helped me pay more attention to the sounds and wildlife around us and to Rufus's reactions to them. He is our fifth Westie (we also have a twelve-year-old female, Maille, who has a pacemaker).
>
> As Macbeth had been getting up in years, I had been preparing myself for his demise. I can't imagine the shock of losing Inka. Please know how much your columns filled with local details mean to dog lovers and Scotland aficionados around the world. May you, the Doyenne and Macbeth share the happy memo-ries of Inka and your walks and may they buoy you in this time of loss.

Hands across the water, you might say!

From the Doyenne's Kitchen

HIGHLAND PHEASANT WITH A
TOUCH OF MANGO

When son Robert was still in the army, he and his family had a holiday house in Portknockie, on the Moray Firth, and daughter-in-law Katie made this delicious dish on one of our visits. I do love roast pheasant – especially a nice young hen – but sometimes you only have large elderly cock pheasants and this is an excellent way to serve them, so I quickly scribbled down her recipe.

Serves 6 to 8
2 pheasants
salt and freshly ground black pepper
2 large onions chopped
2 oz plain flour
1 tablespoon vegetable oil
1 x 250ml carton crème fraiche
4 good tablespoons mango chutney
3 tablespoons Worcestershire sauce
1 small mango chopped or sliced
1 tablespoon fresh parsley

For the stock:
2 sticks celery
1 carrot
1 onion
A few parsley stalks

Method

The day before you need the dish put the pheasants in a casserole with the stock ingredients and seasoning. Cover with cold water and bring slowly to the boil on the hob then simmer in the oven for 1½ to 2 hours at 160 degrees celsius. Leave to cool overnight.

Lift the pheasants from the stock and measure out 8 fl. ozs to add to the sauce. Strip the meat off the pheasants and cut into manageable sized pieces.

Heat the oil, sauté the onions until soft, then add the flour and cook for 2 minutes. Gradually stir in the reserved stock, allow to thicken and stir in the crème fraiche. Add the mango chutney, Worcestershire sauce and seasoning, then the fresh mango and finally the cooked pheasant.

Turn into an ovenproof dish, reheat, garnish with parsley and serve.

NOVEMBER

Winter Visitors

*The dancing lights; burning the hills; massacre on the roads;
the Crystal Causeway; displaced banana; flying squirrels; a
dog's timetable; the robin is still singing; look out for crimson
hawthorn berries – last of the fruits of summer.*

Water of Life

Last week the Doyenne and I headed for a week's break
on the west coast. We were blessed with near perfect
weather – a repeat of the Indian summer I wrote about
a couple of weeks back. It wasn't an action-packed holiday – just days out here and there, as they say in Aberdeen – but there was time to take the dogs on longer
walks than they likely would have got at home.

The dogs and I took ourselves off to walk part-way
down the Craignish Peninsula. You can park the car
beside the old jetty where they used to catch the ferry
to the island of Jura. Macbeth manages well despite

his wee sawn-off legs. Sometimes he has to take the long way round obstacles that Inka leaps over, but he's always game to go any place where there are beckoning smells. I found a comfy hollow in the heather beside the shore and lay there gazing across the sound. In the gap between the islands of Jura and Scarba is the famous Gulf of Corryvreckan, said to be the third largest whirlpool in the world.

To get to Ardmaddy Castle you come off the A816 from Oban to Lochgilphead at Kilninver, and follow the single-track road. Don't take the turning marked Seil Island and Easdale, just carry straight on. The castle sits at the head of a bay enclosed on its three inland sides by wooded cliffs, and its original parts are very old. The woodland walks and formal walled gardens are open to the public and although the best of the flowers were past, the colours of the trees and the sea and the sky made up for it.

The gardens are noted for their collections of rhododendrons and azaleas, and while Scotland's west coast benefits from the warming Gulf Stream we were nonetheless surprised to see some confused rhododendron bushes starting to flower. Local ravens serenaded us with deep throaty 'kronks' as we nodded off in the sun.

Seil really is an island although it's not obvious from the average road atlas. At Clachan, the humpback bridge over the Atlantic crosses a narrow sea channel, which is the most easterly incursion of the Atlantic

Ocean and separates Seil from the mainland. You have the choice of driving to the ferry to Luing Island or, about halfway there, turn right and head west to Easdale Island.

In the 1960s my father owned a cottage on Easdale and he used to tell a wicked story about the ferryman who ran the ferry between Easdale and Seil. The ferryman liked a touch of whisky (Father was well disposed towards it too, I have to say) to keep out the chill sea airs. The easiest way to get rid of the empty bottles was overboard and consequently the strip of water separating the two islands became known as the Crystal Causeway!

Pilgrimage

Glimmering, shimmering, constantly moving like oil upon water, the Aurora Borealis filled our skies last week. It was hardly surprising that the night-time phenomenon was given such national press coverage. It was one of the most spectacular examples of the Northern Lights in memory and such an exciting example of nature's ability to move and inspire our imaginations. Unseen, unearthly power manipulating the skies above us.

I was delighted we had an opportunity to watch it. The Doyenne and I were guests at a very convivial supper party, and before sitting down to eat we went outside to watch the heavens 'declare the wondrous works' – if Handel can forgive my dire paraphrasing. The addition of a glass of wine to protect us from the chill night air contributed to the experience.

Short of disappearing into the trackless parts of Scotland's high hilly places, one of the best spots to watch the skies that evening must have been the Crask Inn in Sutherland. It lies midway between Lairg and Altnaharra on the A836 and is one of the most isolated places I know.

You're into flow country at Crask, which sits on a high plateau surrounded by some pretty rugged mountains, so there's lots of sky. I called proprietors Michael and Kai Geldard who confirmed it had been as spectacular as I had thought it would be. There are no artificial urban lights within ten miles in any direction, so there is a complete absence of orange glow or light pollution on the horizon.

Michael, with whom I once played a rough form of Highland farm cricket, told me the Lights had filled the whole sky. It had not been particularly colourful, mostly a green sensation, indefinably fluid, which illuminated the sky and the hills round about, but the complete suffusion of the visible sky had been its most dramatic feature.

What a welcome sight the Crask Inn must have seemed a hundred years ago when the road would have been a water-bound track and the sense of remoteness more profound. Although, on reflection, perhaps not. Travellers then were better used to the idea of remoteness, but the idea of a welcome dram would likely have helped to hurry their steps along. It's no less welcoming today.

There was a recent TV programme about the mountain rescue dogs of Snowdonia. Macbeth was absolutely riveted. He very quickly notices other dogs on the screen and sits in front of it with his ears cocked up, watching everything that goes on, the very picture of canine alertness.

The temperature has been sub-zero when I've taken Macbeth out last thing, and in the mornings the car has been white with frost. In contrast, by lunchtime the temperature has risen so much that small clouds of mosquitoes have been dancing in the sunny patches in the garden. I doubt if they'll be dancing for too much longer!

Squirrel for Supper

Last Sunday the weather took a turn for the better and I spent much of the day in the garden. The dawn set the standard for the day and by the time Macbeth and I went out for his morning walk the clouds were high in the sky and the sun was shining.

It was rush hour for the geese, and skein after skein passed over us flying west to their feeding grounds. The sun is lower in the sky at this time of year and it caught the birds' light undercarriages. Some of them were so high they seemed set to fly over the Cairn O' Mount. I watched small packs of the birds break away from larger groups and drop onto fields closer by. Away at the end of it all came a single bird, calling constantly in its efforts to keep in contact. How did it let itself get left so far behind?

Fieldfares, and their smaller cousins the redwings, are winter visitors to Britain from Northern Europe. About a dozen of the birds descended on the last of the elderberries and stripped the bushes bare – to the irritation, no doubt, of our resident black-birds. These winter migrants are the same family as thrushes, and the breast feathers of the redwing can be mistaken for a song thrush. However, as soon as it turns side-on and you can see the red patch on its wing – hence the name – any confusion is soon cleared up.

Two small coveys of our own native grey partridges have been working the field edges and roadsides close to the house. Grey partridges have been in decline for a long time so it's a great pleasure to see them. Like hares, they were once so common, and it would be very exciting if they could make a comeback to something like their past numbers.

A dead red squirrel, its body still warm, lay at the side of the road when Macbeth and I went out again for his evening walk. The driver responsible could have taken just a little extra care and avoided the needless death of another of our endangered native animals.

Red squirrels round here appear to be holding their own against the advance of the larger American grey species, introduced into Britain in the 1870s. The greys fight with our native red squirrels and they are carriers of squirrel pox to which they are immune, but against which the reds have no defence.

Conservationists are concerned at the grey's almost complete domination in England and the expansion of its range northwards in Scotland. There seems to be less conflict than usual amongst the conservationists about the trapping and disposal of greys in order to protect our native species. So common are grey squirrels now that they are on sale in butchers' shops in the north of England, and appearing on restaurant menus. The meat is described as moist and sweet because their diet is principally berries and nuts, and is said to taste like a cross between lamb and duck. Free-range, low in fat and low in food miles, they tick all the boxes for healthy eating.

We've seen none of our red squirrels at the feeding table for some weeks. Friends who put out large quantities of peanuts, and had a very busy resident population, report the same sudden drop in visits. They gave me an eyewitness account confirming the depredation of red squirrels by buzzards. They watched fascinated as a buzzard plucked a red squirrel off a high branch of a tree in their garden and flew off with its prey's bushy tail flapping beneath its talons.

That was nature's way, the survival of the fittest – the squirrel's resourcefulness and inherent alertness to danger matched against the bird's hunting skills. Matched against a speeding car the squirrels don't stand a chance and when we're driving on narrow country roads reducing speed by even 10 m.p.h. will increase the squirrels' chances immeasurably.

Our Sunday ended with a really splendid sunset. I sat on a dyke, faithful hound at my feet, just watching nature seep away into the distance, and counted my blessings for being where I was.

Faith Put into Words

'The golden evening brightens in the west' (as the hymnist wrote), sums up several glorious sunsets that the dogs and I enjoyed at the start of the week. I'm no artist, as Colin Gibson, my predecessor in this column was, and I never seem to have the camera with me to record the natural beauty that floods the skies.

How do you compare one sunset with the next? How would you paint a sunset – which is the moment you would want to capture forever? Nature's canvas never stays still, the evening colours constantly blending and melding into one another. You don't see it happening, you just know it has – in the blink of an eye – as the day slips below the western horizon. Perhaps it's the transient moment that lingers longest in the memory.

Walks with the dogs, last thing, have been in bright moonlight, so there's been no need for a torch. Black Inka disappears into the gloom, but he doesn't like to lose contact for too long and soon comes back to reassure me, and himself, that he hasn't got lost. Macbeth poddles on behind appearing like an ectoplasm, as my mother would have said, from hedge bottoms where tantalising scents have delayed him. Tawny owls, of which there are plenty, call all around us. The night time is nearly as busy as the day. Every once in a while a nervous pigeon clatters out of its roost and into the darkness, or a wary cock pheasant 'klokks' a warning to its chums.

We light the sitting-room fire most evenings, which gets Macbeth's vote. He's definitely a heat-seeking missile, and when he no longer has a sheltered corner to bake in the sun, he likes nothing better than to creep as near the fire as possible without actually bursting into flames, and gently toast. He has taken to grooming Inka if it has been raining and we come home wet.

Inka settles down comfortably, thoroughly enjoying the whole process, and Macbeth licks him dry until, I suspect, he runs out of lick!

'But lo, there breaks a yet more glorious day', continues the hymnist in the next verse. Perhaps he was thinking of hillsides ablaze with the glory of the sun. Out with the dogs for the early walk I saw, through a break in the trees, one hillside ablaze. This was 'muirburn', which is the controlled burning carried out by gamekeepers of old heather to improve habitat and grazing for grouse and red deer. When the new growth appears it provides ideal feeding for the grouse whose diet consists mainly of shoots of ling heather.

With the glens of Angus on our doorstep, we don't have to wander far into 'earth's wide bounds' (that hymnist again) to enjoy the sunrises and the sunsets. We're well favoured round here, as my father would have said.

Comforting Glass of Sherry

The eyes caught mine in an unwavering gaze, and my own were drawn to the kitten sitting in the grass, looking very wary about Inka and Macbeth. Neither dog had noticed it but as soon as I stopped they came bounding back to see why. It's remarkable how a wild animal, sitting so still, can demand attention just with its eyes. Obviously the product of a late litter, it was quite ready to defend itself despite its lack of size. It was wild, semi-feral, but certainly not a 'wildcat'. There are only a few hundred true Scottish wildcats left living in out-of-the-way spots, in out-of-the-way glens, well away from human disturbance. So endangered are they that a Scottish Wildcat Association has been launched to promote their interests and protect their future.

The kitten made no attempt to escape and I couldn't make out if it was injured, for it sat hunkered down in the grass like a tabby in front of the fire. It would have nothing to do with Macbeth who was ready for a chat but just got spitting and growls for his pains. I put Inka away – he could have killed it with one bite.

I wondered if this was a repeat of the kitten Holly's story who I found, near dead, on a frozen road on a freezing January morning. I took her to the vet who revived her and she was adopted by one of the veterinary nurses who wrote to me afterwards to say how she had become a much-loved family member. This kitten seemed quite self-assured and perhaps the mother was watching and waiting for us lot to get on our way. Anyway, I left it where it was; if it was suffering, nature usually has a fairly swift remedy in these situations.

I got a call from Rev. Andrew Greaves who was in a state of some outrage which I shared when I heard what he told me. In the space of only a fortnight he had counted five dead red squirrels on the short road connecting the Brechin–Edzell road with the Brechin–

Little Brechin road. A lady from Luthermuir told me she had similarly seen roadkill squirrels on the Lang Stracht, which is the road that runs past the old Edzell US Navy Base.

Squirrels are completely at home in the treetops but on the roadside they get confused by the speed of cars. Reduce your speed and you'll give yourself more time to react to these bonny creatures, and they'll have more time to get out of your way.

The Doyenne has arrived home and announced that it is snowing, which is early, based on the experience of recent years' weather patterns. A warming glass of sherry is just the ticket on these occasions, so I'll need to dash!

Ghost Raiders

Sometimes themes recur. Last week I wrote about barn owls and a couple of days later I was in Morayshire, without dogs for once, which is a part of the country I enjoy visiting, in no small part because of the contrast with the countryside here at home. I was walking in brilliant sunshine on the flat plain beside the coast where the RAF built its two air bases at Lossiemouth and Kinloss.

Later, in the dusk, somewhere between Lossiemouth Air Station and Lhanbryde, which sounds as if it really should be in the depths of Wales. (In the original article in the *Courier* I spelt it 'Llanbryde' and was ticked off for being slack by a regular reader, who grew up near the village. She was quite right to correct me!) I was in a hide beside a pond with the unlikely name of The Banana (which is a little bit surreal) to watch duck flight in. Out of the gloom, flying practically at head level, appeared four short-eared owls. Silent as ghosts, they were past almost as soon as I realised what they were. I can't think that I've seen four all at once hunting as a pack.

Still on the subject of birds of prey a Perthshire farmer told me about two buzzards he came across feeding on a carcass at the road verge. He stopped and the birds were sweir to leave their meal, but flew off when he got out of his car. Their quarry was a hedgehog which they had turned on its back then ripped open its soft underbelly, which is free of spines, and were feeding on the innards.

Some say that buzzards are scavengers and feed only on carrion and never kill prey on the wing. I've heard first-hand reports of buzzards plucking red squirrels from the boughs of trees and stories of them taking pigeons in the air. And red-legged or French partridges are said to be a favourite prey. If the unfortunate hedgehog was a road-kill victim it would support the scavenger hypothesis. If it was attacked going about its lawful business crossing the road, it would bear out the idea that buzzards are raptors. Perhaps, just to confuse us ordinary mortals, they resort to both means of catching their food.

I was shackled to the computer all afternoon until I got a dunt under the elbow from Inka's nose to remind me that time was long overdue for the walk. I poked my own nose out of the door to see the state of the weather and it was pitch dark and sleeting. Preparing for the worst I put on my waxed jacket and climbed into the wellies and the waterproof over-trousers and topped it all with the tweed 'pickiesae'. By the time I'd gone through all this palaver the sleet had stopped, the clouds cleared and we went for a fine walk in bright moonlight with a brisk wind to clear the head.

Folk dream of escaping from the Scottish winters. It's not escaping, it's running away. I wouldn't miss winter in Angus for the world. By way of a postscript, a pickie-sae is the Aberdeenshire name for an item of headgear which my father called a 'fore-and-after' and others call a Sherlock Holmes hat.

From the Doyenne's Kitchen

SAUSAGE PIE

Arriving home from work at around 6.30 p.m. on a raw November evening what we both need is a hot filling dish which can be put on the table quickly. If I remember to phone ahead and ask Angus to put potatoes on to boil it's even quicker. I don't know where this recipe came from but I've been making it for all our married life, maybe even before that.

Serves 2
4 slices Lorne sausage
1 tin baked beans
Mashed potato

Method
Fry the Lorne sausage (or put in the oven for 20 minutes – another job Angus can deal with) until it is cooked, and pour off the fat into your dripping jar and keep for future use.

Flatten and press the sausage into an ovenproof dish so as to cover its base.

Heat the baked beans and pour onto the sausage.

Top with creamy mashed potato (mashing potatoes – another job for husbands!) and dab spots of butter over the potatoes.

Pop into the oven for 10 minutes or until the potato has browned.

Not only is this recipe hot and filling, it's very economical in these credit crunch times.

BANANA MOUSSE

You know how there's always an odd banana that gets left on the fruit bowl until it goes black and no one wants to eat it?

This is a nursery food recipe which I have been using for more than forty years. It continues to be a favourite of our grown-up family and all the grandchildren.

3 very ripe bananas
3 tablespoons lemon juice
3 oz castor sugar
1 small tin evaporated milk
1 sachet powdered gelatine
4 tablespoons water

Method

Put water into a small bowl and sprinkle on the gelatine. Leave to soften then place the bowl in a pan of hot water until the gelatine has completely dissolved.

Place bananas, sugar and lemon juice in food processor and bizz until well liquidised. Adjust the sugar and lemon juice to taste – my family like it quite lemony.

Pour evaporated milk into a bowl and whisk until it has doubled in volume, adding the gelatine mixture gradually while still whisking.

Fold in the banana mixture and pour into a soufflé dish or bowl.

Leave to set and serve with cream.

DECEMBER

Conclusion

Holly berries in abundance hint at a hard winter; death on the roads; nature comes to town; the Doyenne prepares for Christmas; a bit sniffy; flying alert; Big Tree Country; Skon, Skoon or Scone; Rocks of Solitude; what is it if it's not a pigeon; the Doyenne thaws out; on my way to heaven.

Self-destruct Button

Dead roe deer lying at the side of the road are sad testament to the number of these beasts which fail to make it from one side of the road to the other as they cross the path of speeding cars.

My first accident with a roe deer was in the early 1970s in the depths of winter and on an ice-bound road. The deer had lost a foreleg at the knee, and emerging from the side of the road just in front of me it began to hobble across, determined to reach the other side rather than retreat back to the safety of the undergrowth it had just left. If I had slammed on my brakes I might very well have lost control of the car in the icy conditions. Instead I took my foot off the accelerator and hoped I would lose enough headway for the deer to scramble clear.

I reckon it had been caught in a snare which had tightened on its knee and in its efforts to escape it had 'sawn' through the knee joint. If it had had full use of all four legs I'm sure it would have had the agility and speed to escape unscathed. I remember the injury had completely healed, so it had been lame for some time. The deer came from un-keepered woodland, which meant it was likely that the snares were not checked on a daily basis, and while they might have been set for foxes, it may have been a cruel attempt at deer poaching.

Over the years I've encountered a number of these accidents. There is almost a perceived sanctuary on the other side of the road, which the deer *has* to reach, and nothing is going to stop it. It's not only deer – like the apocryphal chicken, pheasants and sheep can display the same blinkered resolve to get to the other side of the road. In their determination to cross at a particular spot, and at a particular moment, they sometimes seem to press a self-destruct button.

Roll on Christmas

Changeable weather seems to be the order of the day

just now. One moment I'm ready to write about the 'iron frost' which greets us in the morning, then a warm front rolls in from the Atlantic and I have to rethink how to start my piece.

You'd expect me to like words, and I always enjoy hearing and using expressions from my childhood that are in danger of being lost to future generations. We Scots have some fine Scotch words, less and less in use nowadays, to describe the weather's fickle moods. Some mornings it's been right rimey when I've walked the dogs in the near frozen mist. The roads have been greasy for driving and I've warned the Doyenne to drop her speed and take care on the corners. Christmas on my own would be no fun.

Other days it's been dreich, mizzling with rain and not been able to make up its mind what it wants to do. The Doyenne has been up to her oxters in preparations for Christmas. The mincemeat is made and the plum puddings are in the making. I look forward to the first batch of mince pies, still warm from the oven and comfortingly full of cholesterol! The turkey is ordered and shortly we'll be collecting the Christmas tree.

Nature isn't just a countryside experience. So long as there is sufficient food to support them, wild animals and birds will be attracted to the city life. Business has taken me to Dundee more than usual recently, and I've been hearing about the peregrines that are seen about the city. The urban environment provides a ready food supply of small mammals and birds which attracts these handsome raptors to the city life. Foxes, possibly the best adaptors in the animal world to city life, are regularly spotted during daylight hours sneaking through the Eastern Cemetery.

Dundee is fortunate to have gardens, parks and other green places such as the airport and the Observatory Hill at Balgay where wildlife can flourish. The Dundee Botanic Garden, which belongs to Dundee University, is a gem of a small botanic garden and an asset and resource which should be valued and supported by Dundonians. And not forgetting the ponds at Camperdown and Caird Park, and the reservoir at Clatto, the seashore and the River Tay. Grey seals are regularly seen at low tide on the sandbanks above the railway bridge. Even the two bridges themselves, carrying the railway and the road, provide overnight roosting places for birds, and the foundations of their piers and pillars provide an ideal environment for submarine species like mussels, limpets and crabs. Yes, Dundee provides habitats for as wide a range and diversity of wildlife as any country lover would hope to see.

A Bit Sniffy

I came across a startling fact – that a dog's sense of smell is 300–400 times keener than that of us humans.

I know what a smelly little tyke Macbeth can be sometimes. Heaven only knows what he thinks of me. I'm just thankful the Doyenne is fragrant.

David Douglas Grows on You

The sun is low in the sky at this time of year. On bright mornings when I escape into my office I need to close the curtains, otherwise the sun shining in through the window completely obscures my computer screen. And the glare of the low setting sun in the afternoons sometimes makes driving difficult on winding country roads. Why do I complain? Many's another day the sun doesn't show itself and it's almost dark by half past three.

An appointment in Blairgowrie at half past eight meant an early start. The sun was up as I turned off the A94 at Coupar Angus and headed up the A923 to Blair. On the outskirts of Coupar Angus is a house called 'Boatlands' overlooking the River Isla. (In the original article I referred to the River Ericht and was corrected by an observant reader. I never mind being taken to task for my silly errors, and do my best now to check out facts before I impetuously commit things to print). Each time I pass it I wonder whether there may have been a ferry crossing there before the bridge was built several hundred yards further upstream.

The river at this point flows wide and slow, and

as I drove over the bridge a swan was making heavy weather of getting off the water and into full flight. They are somewhat clumsy creatures until properly airborne, and this one was having difficulty dodging round the traffic crossing the bridge. It appeared to fly straight at the pickup in front of me before taking urgent evasive action and scraping over the top of the pickup and my own car. A bit scary for the driver to see so large a bird about to land in his lap! And I imagine it jangled the swan's nerves as well.

Driving through Scone on the homeward journey from Perth, I noticed yet again the sign to the David Douglas Memorial. I can't say how often I'd seen the sign and promised myself that one day I would take a look at it. It was a sunny afternoon, so I decided to investigate. The memorial is in Scone (pronounced Skoon) Old Parish Kirkyard and commemorates the celebrated plant hunter David Douglas, who started his working life as an apprentice gardener at the age of eleven on the Scone Estate.

By the time he died in 1834 at the age of thirty-five he had explored much of the American Pacific Northwest and the Columbia River. It was he who introduced those magnificent trees – Douglas firs (named after him of course) to Britain. Perthshire is called the Big Tree Country and surely the Douglas firs planted by the Victorians, who followed David Douglas, have contributed to this characterisation of the county.

In his short life of exploration David Douglas sent

home more than 200 flowers, shrubs and trees, including the sitka spruce, another tall and graceful conifer, as well as lupins, Rose of Sharon, sun-flowers and monkey flowers. I didn't know such a famous Scot had grown up in Scone. Knew nothing about the importance of his contribution to our woodlands and gardens. So I'm glad my curiosity got the better of me.

It must be confusing for visitors. They stop for a break in Perth and eat a 'skon' with jam and butter. Leaving the Fair City they ask the way to 'Skon' because they would like to pay their own homage to the great explorer, but get directed to 'Skoon' instead.

Solitude

A southerly wind was blowing an already high tide higher up the beach. A fine mist of spray from breaking seas on the rocky shore at the top end of St Cyrus Bay cast a veil over the cliff tops at the edge of the village. It was a coorse sort of morning as I parked at Scottish Natural Heritage's Nature Reserve Centre at Nether Warburton, but I needed to see the sea. (Take the A92 coast road from Montrose to Aberdeen and immediately after crossing the Lower Northwaterbridge – over the River North Esk – turn right under the disused railway viaduct and follow the single track road for about a mile to the nature reserve car park).

A wooden bridge to the sand dunes crosses over the former bed of the River North Esk, which previously flowed into the North Sea about half a mile further north than today. Years ago, during an especially wild storm, shifting sand blocked the original channel and the river changed its course to its present outfall. There's been a bridge there for as long as I can remember, but the old one fell into disrepair and lost so many planks that it became a danger to walkers and was replaced some years back by volunteers from the Ghurka regiments.

I found a sheltered spot, out of the wind, and spent a little time with my own thoughts. The waves were short and close together. As each one broke it met the backwash of the one before it, and they chased each other until their energy was spent. The sound of the water drowned out the noise of the wind and I sat, mesmerised by the constant motion, shut away in my own wee buckie shell.

The horizon was low and raw-looking and I wished I'd remembered to take my cap. Beneath the sluicing sound of the sea was the constant, dull roar of a relentless energy, which rose from the seabed as if powered by some monstrous submarine engine.

In the afternoon, I took the dogs up the riverside walk through the Blue Door at the Gannochy Bridge which crosses the North Esk just above Edzell. The river had risen considerably with several days heavy rain and was fairly rammling through the Gannochy Gorge as it fought its way to the sea. I was cocooned by the white noise of impatient water rattling past in a rare state of aggravation. Even the normally tranquil pools at the upper beat of The Burn fishing water were hurrying on their way. We walked as far as the Rocks of Solitude, and stopped where the water fell into a black pot with a roar like a jet from RAF Leuchars passing low over the house.

They say the Rocks are so called because you can't hear your companion speaking above the noise of the rushing water and are overcome by a sense of solitude. When I spoke to my companions, they looked back and wagged their tails! 'Money will buy a pretty good dog,' the saying goes, 'but it won't buy the wag of its tail.' With two dogs for companions there's no place for solitude.

First Sighting

It's almost five years since I began writing these Saturday pieces (first article appeared on 4 January 2003) and I've had some wonderful encounters with nature. Knowing I've had a weekly column to fill and a deadline to meet has made me more conscious of what goes on around me when the dogs and I set out each afternoon. I'm always on the lookout for things to write about; sometimes I've been in the right place at the right time and sometimes it's been sheer good luck – as happened last Sunday.

The urgent tone of the Doyenne's summons alerted me that something pretty special was happening and I raced downstairs as fast as I could – which is not quite as speedy as it used to be! I joined her peering out of the kitchen window and my first response was to wonder what all the fuss was about, for all I could see was a pigeon on the path outside apparently feeding on the discards from the bird table, but the lower part of its body was obscured by the leaves of a fern.

A tremendous commotion of frightened squawks had caught the Doyenne's attention and she had looked out of the window to see the bird standing with its wings outstretched, like a cape or a mantle, over something which was obscured by the wings. It's what birds of prey do to stop their prey escaping and it's called 'mantling'.

My pigeon turned its head and looked me in the eye from scarcely eight feet away, and it took a moment or two for the penny to drop. This was an altogether bolder bird than a pigeon. Its head was clearly smaller than a pigeon's and no pigeon ever had a short, curved beak like the bird below me.

From its slate grey back plumage I realised I was looking at a male merlin, which is our smallest hawk, and this was the first time I'd seen one in the wild.

I could see that he was holding something in his talons which he was tearing at. He looked up at me several times without any hint of fear, almost as if saying: 'Can't a chap enjoy his lunch in peace?'

I can't think what possessed me to open the kitchen door to see if I could get a better look at what he had taken, but that was too much for him and he shot into a nearby beech tree, taking the dead blackbird with him. With a little patience we might have seen so much more!

I've always associated merlins with moors and open spaces rather than woodlands, but we're on the march of the glen and the woods and the songbirds at the bird table provide a ready source of food for hungry raptors.

It was truly exciting and I wonder if I'll see a wild bird of prey going about its business quite so close again. (As a footnote to that story I've seen a merlin three times since, within about half a mile of the house).

Frozen in Time

The Doyenne took one of her turns this week. I blame myself; I saw it coming and should have done more to help, but probably nothing I could have said would have changed things. She decided to clear out and defrost the deep freeze.

It's anxious times when she gets these notions because she gets quite cross about the things she finds that should have been used years ago. A pair of kippers from November 2005, rhubarb from the last century tucked away into a corner, the frost-burnt lamb chops that fell out of the packet and aren't fit to eat now. And of course there was the mole that I put in a poly-bag to show the grandchildren and forgot all about!

But some good came out of it after all. There were strawberries and gooseberries and, thrifty Yorkshire girl that she is, she couldn't bear to put them in the bin. Before you could say 'Grand Old Duke' she had the jam pan out, and for a couple of evenings the kitchen was filled with the tantalising smell of strawberry jam and gooseberry jelly, which smelt the sweeter for being made when it was so cold and frosty outside. On a more practical note for jam makers, La D. commented that both had set much more quickly than usual. She wondered if freezing the fruit breaks down the pectin, or if it had anything to do with the fruit being put on to boil while it was still frozen.

The bottle of gin I had my eye on disappeared off the shelf. She had found three bags of sloes and before I could say 'Gay Gordons' she had the lot bottled up for sloe gin. It's a pity she hadn't found them a couple of months earlier and we could have greeted the New Year with our home-made hedgerow cordial. Instead, we'll drink the raspberry vodka which must be just about ready for sampling.

Out early with the dogs – about half past eight actually, but still so dark it felt early – I was looking for holly to 'deck the halls', but the growth is very disappointing compared with last year when the branches were dripping with berries. Macbeth's hunting instincts were aroused when a field vole, otherwise known as the short-tailed vole, made a dash across the track to the safety of the undergrowth on the other side. They are one of the countryside's commonest small rodents and move at a tremendous pace for such small animals. They like sweet, young grass and there's not much about at this time of year, so they are constantly on the move in their day-long quest for food.

We disturbed a cock pheasant which flew out of its roost high up in a pine tree with loud 'klokks' of indignation. Before I knew what, all the pheasants in the neighbourhood had chimed in and were expressing their disapproval at the early reveille . . .

Dismissal

Last Saturday night was a night of such purity and clarity that if I hadn't believed in a God and thought I would like to, there was no better moment I could think of to make a start.

The dogs and I were out for their last run before bed. A full moon and distant stars shone from the infinite oblivion of the midnight sky, bouncing off the grass, the branches, the walls and the roof slates which were covered in a hard white frost, almost as if there had been a fall of snow.

I stood in the bell-mouth of a field gate enveloped by the white sound of nothing, for there was no wind to stir even the topmost branches of the leafless trees. The dogs decided they had been sitting patiently long enough and started scratting around in the dead leaves, and that broke the spell.

You can't recreate silent beauty like that. It's difficult to catch moments of such complete peace when people and traffic and the whole business of living are constantly on the move. The Doyenne joined me when we got back and we stood in the garden looking in at our Christmas tree covered in its lights and shining out from the darkened drawing room. It felt like the spirit of Christmas.

Three weeks ago, I was asked by the congregation of Dundee West Church to join them at their morning service and take part in a conversation with their minister, Rev. Andrew Greaves. He had chosen the themes of preservation and conservation of what is good about Christmas, and related them to the landscape we live in.

It was a great compliment to think that some of the things I've written about have struck enough of a chord to merit being talked about again. I've never thought of this column as having a spiritual resonance but if going into the countryside brings peace and comfort then it is one of the best reasons to protect it for our benefit and enjoyment.

I found myself having to justify myself to myself, as well as to the congregation, and tell them, publicly, about the personal things I care for. Regeneration of the countryside which man has harmed and destroyed is as important as conserving what is already good. We need to acknowledge what we have done to our world and decide what we are prepared to do to pass on a sustainable world to the generations who follow.

I'm not giving advance notice of anything when I end this piece with a prayer by St Thomas More – it's just the nicety of his language. I think he's saying that caring for each other is one of the ways we can achieve happiness, and that's pretty important in life: 'Pray for me, as I will for thee, that we may merrily meet in Heaven.'

From the Doyenne's Kitchen

NEWTON MILL TERRINE

The shooting season is in full swing by this time of year and wild pheasant is readily available in many butchers' shops until the end of January. With Christmas and New Year celebrations to think of, and other seasonal entertaining, I like to have a tasty terrine in the larder. This recipe comes from our friend Rose Rickman and is economical and makes one pheasant go a long way. It is also an ideal way of stretching out that forgotten single pheasant that you find in the deep freeze in the middle of summer.

You will need:

An earthenware or cast iron terrine with lid, or a loaf tin lined with baking parchment. (If using an earthenware or cast iron terrine there is no need to line it with parchment paper.)

1 bay leaf

8 rashers smoked bacon
1 cup fresh white breadcrumbs
1 onion chopped and softened in a little butter
1 teaspoon fresh thyme or a good pinch of dried
1 clove garlic, crushed
1½ lb minced pork
Strips of poached pheasant breast
1 large egg or 2 small (enough to bind well)
Salt and fresh ground pepper

Method

Place the bay leaf in the centre of the dish. Line the dish neatly with the bacon rashers.

In a bowl mix all the ingredients except the pheasant strips. Bind the mixture with the egg.

Half-fill the dish with the pork mixture. Carefully lay the pheasant strips on top and press firmly onto the mixture. Add the rest of the pork mixture. Smooth off and fold any ends of bacon rashers over the mixture. Cover with terrine lid.

If using a loaf tin place a piece of baking parchment over the mixture and then cover again tightly with tin foil to form a tightly sealed lid.

Place in a bain-marie and poach gently for 1 to 1½ hours.

Remove and allow to cool. Replace the tin foil and leave for 24 hours to set and mature. Using a flat knife turn out carefully onto an oblong dish. Cut into slices to serve.

Instead of pheasant you can use chicken, grouse or pigeon.

CHRISTMAS IN A GLASS

Determined to be the embodiment of country living our daughter Cait invented her special Christmas liqueur. Its main ingredient is supermarket blueberries and when I queried why she hadn't been true to her aspirations and gone into the hills and glens to pick true Scottish blaeberries, the best she could come up with was that it was closed season for blaeberries, and anyway what she wanted to do was make cheap vodka taste better. Not for the first time I was unable to follow her logic, but one thing is certain, the resultant cordial is very delicious and Christmas is a very good time to drink it.

75 cl bottle with a cork (e.g. whisky or sherry bottle)
Enough blueberries to half-fill the bottle
Enough sugar to cover the blueberries
Rind of 1 lemon
5 cloves

2 peppercorns
2 thick or 4 thin cinnamon sticks
Enough cheap vodka to fill the bottle

Method

Put the cinnamon sticks into the bottle. Peel thin strips of lemon rind with a vegetable peeler. Pierce each berry with a sharp knife before popping it into the bottle. Then add cloves, peppercorns and lemon peel. Pour the sugar over the berries until it has permeated to the bottom of the jar, all the gaps are filled and the sugar just covers the berries and no more. Pour the vodka over everything and cork the bottle. Shake gently to dissolve the sugar – don't go mad or the fruit will bruise. Put the bottle into the store cupboard and every day or so give it a shoogle (Scottish for 'shake'). It should be ready to drink in a month. When I first made it I had no idea what to expect so just before Christmas we opened it – just to test of course! – to see how it was getting on. It was 'Christmas in a Glass', every flavour you associate with Christmas was there. The most festive thing I'd ever tasted and it really put me in the Christmas mood.

Strain before drinking just as much as you need – or, if it's for a gift, strain and return to a clean bottle.

A Very Happy Christmas.